To My
Hope

Astronauts, Athletes, & Ambassadors

Oklahoma Women from 1950 –2007

By Glenda Carlile

HERNDON 2006

Glenda Carlile
5 – 2017

NEW FORUMS
Stillwater, Oklahoma
U.S.A.

NEW FORUMS PRESS INC.

Published in the United States of America
by New Forums Press, Inc.
1018 S. Lewis St.
Stillwater, OK 74074
www.newforums.com

Library of Congress Cataloging-in-Publication Data
Pending

This book may be ordered in bulk quantities at dis-
count from New Forums Press, Inc., P.O. Box 876,
Stillwater, OK 74076 [Federal I.D. No. 73 1123239].
Printed in the United States of America.

International Standard Book Number: 1-58107-125-6

Edited by Carolyn D. Wall.

Cover design by Mark Herndon.

First paperback edition / 1 2 3 4 5 6 7 8 9 0

Praise for Astronauts, Athletes, & Ambassadors

"In her own eloquent style, Glenda Carlile relays the important impact women have made on the state of Oklahoma, the nation, and the world. With a sense of style and grace, many of these women achieved success, at a time in society, when equality of opportunity was not afforded every American. Exemplifying a spirit that is uniquely Oklahoma, they continue to serve as positive role models for other women."

Connie Armstrong
Editor, *Oklahoma Almanac*

"I think the women Glenda Carlile has chosen to profile in this book all have that hallmark of striving to be the best in their field. From each of these women, readers can draw strength from their experiences. All have ridden the merry-go-round of highs and lows in their life. All have known joys and setbacks. What characterizes each one was their ability to handle changes in their lives and their communities and strive to make a difference in their world. The women gathered on these pages can serve as a beacon of hope to others for their exemplary examples of courage and leadership. Their stories may have their genesis in a different era, but they are still inspiring role models for today's generations to follow."

M. J. VanDeventer
Editor, *Persimmon Hill Magazine*

"These were ordinary women who, through genetics, environment, or pure stubbornness, created for themselves extraordinary situations. They listened to their hearts, made eyes-open decisions, and drove into their futures without looking back."

Carolyn D. Wall

The Write Page, Inc.

Acknowledgements

Oklahoma will be celebrating the state's centennial in 2007. The celebration of 100 years of history is an exciting time for all Oklahomans.

From the beginning, women have been a part of this incredible story. In *Buckskin, Calico, and Lace,* I wrote about the territorial women and in *Petticoats, Politics, and Pirouettes,* I featured the women who made contributions from 1900 to 1950.

Now, in *Astronauts, Athletes, and Ambassadors,* I have had the pleasure of writing about the accomplishments of Oklahoma women from 1950 to 2007. I recall many of the actual events that took place during this time and have had the opportunity to visit with some of these women that I have admired through the years. I thank them for their accomplishments and sharing their memories.

I was fortunate to have access to the Oklahoma Room at the Oklahoma Department of Libraries, the Oklahoma History Center, The Oklahoma Heritage Association, and the fine local libraries and museums across the state.

Many people have offered their historical expertise and/or encouragement including Bob Blackburn, Bill Welge, Rodger Harris, and Judith Michener from the Oklahoma History Center; Ginny Campbell from the Oklahoma Heritage Association; Kitty Pittman, Connie Armstrong and the Bills (Bill Petrie, Bill Young, and Bill Struby) from the Oklahoma Department of Libraries, and Blake Edwards and Jeanie Edney with the Oklahoma Centennial Commission.

I appreciate the help and support of Molly Levite Griffis, Bob Burke, Eric Dabney, Jennifer

Paustenbaugh, Nancy DeQuevedo, Linda Stempert, the One Plus Class, and my Southern Hills Friends.

A book that I have used and found invaluable is the *Oklahoma Womens Almanac* by Robert Darcy and Jennifer Paustenbaugh, published by the Governor's Commission on the Status of Women and Oklahoma State University.

Supporting this project has been my critique group; the Dead Writers Society: Judy Gigstad, Laurette Hager, Gary Johnson, Dottie Hall, Keith Myers, Shirley Pritchett, Shirley Trochta, Maria Veres, and Carolyn Wall. Also the ATOGS (All the Old Gals) the best group of friends anyone could have. They are: Micky Balog, Geri Campbell, Ann Carter, Linda Egle, Marilyn Geiger, Roberta Henson, Reba Hubbard, JoAnn Hunter, Melaney Mathis, Pat Molnar, Sue Stees, and Myrna Wetzel; Thanks for listening.

I am grateful for the fine work of editor Carolyn D.Wall, artist Mark Herndon, and publisher Douglas Dollar.

Most of all, I extend my most sincere appreciation to my family: my husband Tom, my daughters and their husbands Kim and Jay Williamson, Stacey and Rob Shofner, Margaret Carlile, and my dad Glenn Horn. Also, my grandchildren who constantly provide inspiration; Jayson, Ryane, and Cooper Williamson and Jackson and Olivia Shofner.

Contents

Foreword

Office of the First Lady
Kim Henry

Glenda Carlile's *Astronauts, Athletes and Ambassadors: Oklahoma Women from 1950 to 2007* is a wonderful account of some of the legendary Oklahoma women whose strength, courage and determination continue to serve as an inspiration for us all. In this energetic and entertaining volume, Glenda profiles a number of remarkable women — Shannon Lucid, Clara Luper, Wilma Mankiller, Shannon Miller and Donna Nigh, to name a few -who helped shape our state and nation. In doing so, Glenda Carlile justly honors these exceptional women.

This book is for my mother who always believed in
me~ Alda Horn, 1917-2006

and for Margaret, my assistant, advisor, daughter,
and friend.

Other Books by the Author

*Buckskin, Calico and Lace: Oklahoma's Territorial
Women*

*Petticoats, Politics and Pirouettes: Oklahoma Women
from 1900 to 1950*

*Co-authored with Bob Burke
Kate Barnard, Oklahoma's Good Angel*

*Co-authored with Liz Codding
Oklahoma Yesterday, Today and Tomorrow
Calendars of historic and current events
Volume I –1993
Volume II- 1994
Volume III- 1995*

Jerrie Cobb

Top Women Pilot

Considered the nation's top woman pilot, in 1959, Jerrie Cobb was chosen as the first woman to undergo astronaut testing. Passing with flying colors, Jerrie trained to become the first woman to fly in space. Promised an early flight, NASA appointed her as a consultant to the space program. However, politics entered the space race and it was decided, at that time, to send only males into orbit. Since then, Jerrie Cobb has been flying in the jungles of the Amazon as a missionary bush pilot, providing a link between the natives and the outside world . She has been nominated for a Nobel Peace Prize.

Jerrie Cobb cannot remember a time she did not want to fly. As the daughter of a retired Air Force Colonel, she came by her passion for aviation naturally. On March 5, 1931, in Norman, Oklahoma, Geraldyn M., a name she never uses, Cobb entered the world. Her parents, Lt. Col. William H. Cobb and Helena Butler Stone Cobb were students at the University of Oklahoma.

Born during the depression, her family moved frequently in search of better jobs. At just three weeks old, Jerrie traveled by train to Washington, D.C. In the next few years they moved to Okmulgee, Oklahoma, back to Norman and then to Oklahoma City. These early moves may have contributed to her later wanderlust.

As a National Guardsman, and a member of the 45th Division, her father commanded Company C Engineers and was one of the unit's champion marksmen. By 1938, there were rumblings of war and her father's unit was called to active duty. During World War II, Jerrie and her sister grew up on various military bases. She and her sister Carolyn were known as "army brats" moving from camp to fort to base. Later her family relocated to Ponca City.

Carolyn and Jerrie shared a bedroom. Carolyn's side displayed dolls while Jerrie's was full of model airplanes. Jerrie, also had a speech impediment that required surgery when she was five years old.

She learned to fly at the age of twelve with her father as her flight instructor. He fashioned 12-inch wooden blocks on the rubber pedals and added extra seat cushions to his Waco biplane to compensate for her lack of height.

Jerrie soloed in March, 1947, at the age of sixteen. She spent the next year financing advanced lessons with a variety of odd jobs, including berry picking, waiting tables, training horses, selling tickets at a movie theater, and typing. She waxed all-metal Cessnas at the local airport in return for an hour's flying time.

Her favorite job was barnstorming across the Great Plains as the flying advance person for a circus. She flew low over the small towns dropping flyers advertising the one- elephant circus's scheduled appearance. Then on the day of the show she gave free rides to the town's dignitaries. Nights were spent in a farmer's field sleeping in a bedroll, under the wings of the plane.

On her seventeenth birthday Jerrie received her private pilot's license, and she earned her commercial pilot's license on her eighteenth birthday.

She attended the Oklahoma College for Women in Chickasha briefly but decided to pursue flying full time. Jerrie played three seasons of soft-

Jerrie Cobb, America's top woman pilot. Photo, Courtesy of the Jerrie Cobb Foundation.

ball for the "Sooner Queens," a semiprofessional women's softball team and worked on a horse ranch in Colorado for $5 a week to earn enough money to buy her first plane.

The first plane she owned was an old war surplus Fairchild PT -23 trainer. To support it, she took numerous jobs, including flying crop dusters and pipeline control. She flew low over oil pipelines in Oklahoma, Missouri, and Kansas looking for leaks. Often the work was part-time until a "real pilot," a male, could be hired.

This was a tough time to begin a flying career as World War II had ended and thousands of military pilots were looking for the few civilian jobs available.

Jerrie received her flight instructor's certificate in 1952, on her twenty-first birthday. This enabled her to take a job as an instructor at an airport in Duncan, Oklahoma. Then, the Oklahoma City Downtown Airpark hired her as a flight instructor, pilot for hire, and airport restaurant waitress.

That same year, she placed fourth in her first national event, the Transcontinental Air Race. In June 1953, she placed fourth in the International Women's Air Race.

She applied for a DC-3 co-pilot position at Miami International Airport and was told, "If you really want to fly, try the stewardess office down the hall."

Jerrie met Jack Ford, president of Fleetway Ferry Service, who was looking for pilots to ferry planes to South America. This involved ten day round-trips over uninhabited jungles, ocean, and the Andes Mountains. Male pilots were not interested in the dangerous work, so Ford reluctantly hired Jerrie. It was during this time she became aware of the hopeless isolation of the Amazon Indians.

On one trip, when she landed for fuel in Ecuador, she was arrested as a spy. Fortunately, The United States government arranged for her release but not until she had spent twelve days in jail.

After two years of flying to South America, she was reassigned to fly World War II Surplus bombers from the United States to France. She left Fleetway in 1956, to work as a test pilot in Burbank, California.

That same year, Jerrie was invited by the editor of the *Daily Oklahoman and Times* to publicize the Oklahoma Semi-Centennial Exposition by breaking aviation records in an Oklahoma-built airplane. She accepted.

Jerrie was a woman to be watched in aviation circles. In 1957, she set the world record for non-stop distance in an Aero Commander, flying 1,504 miles from Guatemala City to Oklahoma City. Three weeks later, she set an altitude record by climbing to 30,361 feet in a Commander. That same year she set a class speed record of 226.148 miles per hour and in 1960 bettered her own altitude record by climbing to 37,010 feet in an Aero Commander manufactured in her home state.

After she had applied many times, the company hired her as a test pilot. Her official job for Aero Commander was to attend the World Congress of Flight in Las Vegas in April, 1959. To show off the plane's potential, Jerrie established a new world's speed record for the 2,000-kilometer closed course. She flew the course in 5 hours, 29 minutes, 27 seconds.

Still in her twenties, the Government of France honored Jerrie, as the first woman awarded the Gold Wings of the Federation Aeronautique International. She is one of only a few Americans to be given an award by this international flying organization. In 1957, she received the Amelia Earhart Gold Medal of Achievement by the Ninety-nines, an International Society of Women Pilots. In 1959, Jerrie was named, Pilot of the Year by the National Pilots Association and Woman of the Year by the Women's National Aeronautic Association. She was also one of nine women selected by *Life Magazine* as the "100 most important young people in the United States."

In the infancy of the space age, in September 1959, Jerrie met Dr. Randolph Lovelace, chairman of the National Aeronautics and Space Administration (NASA) Life Sciences Committee for Project Mercury. Studies had been done on the Mercury astronaut, and he wanted to study the effects of space flight on women. He asked Jerrie to be his first subject. She enthusiastically agreed.

This attractive, five foot, seven inch, 124 pound, twenty-eight year old female took the same grueling test as the ones given to the seven Mercury astronauts. On each test, Jerrie matched or bettered the men's statistics. During the isolation test, she was immersed to her neck in an underground water tank. She stayed there for 9 hours, 40 minutes, exceeding the highest of the male tests by more than three hours.

NASA promised her an early space flight, and appointed her a consultant to the space program. She was asked not to tell about the project, but word leaked out, and she was swamped with publicity. She spent her free time giving speeches for NASA to civic groups around the country.

Twelve other females passed the test, and the women became known as the Mercury 13. However, they couldn't overcome the gender barrier and were grounded for three years when politics again became involved. Jerrie continued to train while awaiting her assignment.

In September, 1962, *Life* magazine included Jerrie in it's "100 Outstanding Members of the Take Over Generation," the most important young men and women in the United States.

In 1963, Jerrie was called to testify at a Congressional hearing concerning the inclusion of women in the astronaut corp. She said she found it unbelievable when astronaut John Glenn, the first man to orbit the earth testified that, "Men go off and fight the wars and fly the airplanes," and women are not astronauts because of our social order."

Testimony included test results and reports from scientists and doctors. There were sound medical-scientific reasons for using women as astronauts. Women weighed less and consumed less food and oxygen, were more radiation-resistant and less prone to heart attacks. Scientists had proved that women are less susceptible to monotony, loneliness, heat, cold, pain and noise. Jerrie also noted that the Mercury 13 had an average of 4500 flying hours while the male astronauts had 2500 hours.

Nevertheless, Congress determined that women were not fit to fly in space. They required that astronauts have military jet test pilot experience, but women were not permitted to fly military jets, the only way they could obtain that experience.

A few months later, Russia astounded the world by sending the first woman, Valentina Tershkova, a factory worker, into space.

Jerrie was crushed. The Unites States simply was not ready to include women in its program. NASA did not hire the first female astronauts until 1972, twelve years later. That first class included Oklahoman, Shannon Lucid.

Jerrie, now thirty-two, resigned her position and flew to an area almost as remote as the moon – the Amazon jungle, where she has remained for over forty-two years. As a bush pilot-missionary, she has conducted humanitarian aid missions to the peoples of the Amazon rain forest in six South American nations. She lives with the primitive villagers, sleeping in hammocks under a communal shelter, bathing in rivers, and eating the food they hunted in the jungles. She flies in antibiotics and sometimes seeds. Friends formed the non-profit Jerrie Cobb Foundation to support her missionary work.

In 1964, she was given pilot captain wings, the first civilian ever given rank in the Colombian Air Force. She was presented an airline transport jet pilots license by the Government of Ecuador and honored for "pioneering new air routes over the Andes Mountains and Amazon jungle." The governments of France, Brazil, Columbia and Peru also honored Jerrie for "humanitarian flying serving primitive tribes." The government of France honored her for "outstanding flights serving isolated peoples." For her humanitarian work in the Amazon jungle, she was nominated for the Nobel Peace Prize.

President Nixon, at a white house ceremony, in 1979, presented Jerrie with the Harmon International Trophy for "top woman pilot" in the world. In 1979 she received the Bishop Wright Air Industry Award for her "humanitarian contributions to modern aviation". She was also honored, in 1986, by the Amazonas Comisaria for "life-saving jungle flights".

Not forgotten by her home state, Jerrie received the Pioneer Woman Award for her "courageous frontier spirit" serving primitive Indians. In 1990, she was inducted into the Oklahoma Aviation and Space Hall of Fame, and in 2000 was inducted into the Women in Aviation International Pioneer Hall of Fame.

All these awards have not made up for the dream that Jerrie still has of flying into space. In the spring of 1998, NASA announced that Senator John Glenn, a former astronaut, would join a space shuttle crew the following October. Immediately, special interest groups and individuals across the United States petitioned Congress to send Jerrie Cobb on her first flight, the one she had missed thirty-five years earlier.

Jerrie was in the Amazon and, at first, didn't know about this campaign. When she was contacted and asked by supporters for her permission to conduct the campaign, she couldn't say "yes" fast enough. In a 1990 interview with Anne DeFrange in the *Oklahoman*, Jerrie said, "It's a dream I've held onto for 40 years...and it just might be coming true. Its just part of being a pilot. I've always wanted to fly farther, higher, faster, or out into space".

The National Organization for Women collected signatures on a petition to pressure NASA to permit Jerrie to take part in the same type of space-and-aging studies Glenn is pursuing. Their claim was that if Glenn deserved a second chance, former trainee Jerrie Cobb , a decade younger than Glenn, deserved her first. Joining the campaign was the National Women's History Project, the American Association of University Women of California as well as the United States Senators from Oklahoma and California. Tee- shirts and hats announced "Women Fly". People stood in line to sign petitions.

Newspapers across the country favored Jerrie's cause. The *Boston Herald* printed, "Jerrie Cobb trained as one of America's original astronauts, until NASA decided only men were fit for space exploration." The *Associated Press* commented, "If NASA wants to study the effects of space travel on aging, then it is imperative to make these studies on women. After all, women are the majority of the study." *Florida Today* said, "It's time for NASA to right that wrong. It's time to let Jerrie Cobb fly in space."

NASA Administrator Daniel Goldin said, "It's logical that a woman will be next and there is no one in America more qualified and deserving to be in that space shuttle than Jerrie Cobb."

Jerrie met with John Glenn and congratulated him. She asked him for his support, but he evaded her question. She said she was not angry. "John's just John," she said of her fellow pilot. She had kept up with her training, and she was ready. Summoned to NASA, Jerrie's hopes were deflated when she was told they already had enough astronauts.

Ten years later, in 2006, at age 75, Jerrie is still in the Amazon jungles of South America where she continues flying every day, serving the primitive tribes of the headwaters. She has still not been selected for that flight in space that she longs for. But it takes faith to fly, and she has faith that someday this dream will come true.

Bertha Teague

The Winningest Coach in the Nation

Oklahoma is known for producing superstar coaches – Bud Wilkinson, Barry Switzer, Bob Stoops, Henry Iba, and Abe Lemons. But the coach that won more games than any other was a woman basketball coach from the small town of Byng, Oklahoma. Bertha Teague is known as the winningest ever coach in the nation, in any sport and in any level of competition. One of the first three women inducted into the basketball Hall of Fame, she recorded an incredible 1,157 win and 115 loss record in a glorious span between 1926 and 1969. Bertha Teague coached the Byng Lady Pirates to eight state championships and seven runners-up. Her team went through a 27-year unbeaten streak in conference action. Yet this lady called Mrs. Basketball never played a game herself.

Driving into the town of Byng, Oklahoma, population 1088 one immediately realizes something is different. Ah, yes, every house has a basketball hoop either attached to the house or in the yard.

It's not a big town. The city hall is located in the fire station and there's a small gas station that serves as the general store. A sign on the highway points the way to Byng Schools. The second surprise is that Byng schools are comprised of several buildings on a campus that would rival many state junior colleges. Of the two gymnasiums the oldest one is called the Bertha Frank Teague Gymnasium. Lining the foyer of the gym are glass-enclosed shelves holding trophies presented to the Byng Girls Basketball team and its coach, the famed Bertha Teague. In the alumni room, in another building, are more trophies, pictures of her winning teams, the uniforms she designed for her players, scrapbooks, newspaper articles, and a copy of the book she wrote. This shrine is history of a 43-year coaching career that produced eight state championships. Although Bertha Teague died in 1991 at the age of ninety-two, her legend lives on.

In the foreword to *Basketball for Girls*, authored by Mrs. Teague, Ernest Thompson, sports Editor of the Ada Evening News writes, "The name 'Teague' and the word 'Basketball' are virtually synonymous terms in Oklahoma. In the past 35 years, Mrs. Bertha Frank Teague and her Byng High School Girls have become legend in the southwest. Byng (pronounced Bing is a small school located just north of Ada, Oklahoma. But, its fame in basketball is not compatible with its size."

Ray Soldan, correspondent for the Daily Oklahoman wrote in a 1991 article, "It was with pride that Bertha Frank Teague was always quick to point out that she'd never played a game of basketball in her life. But basketball was the life of the super successful coach"

"You don't have to play basketball or any other kind of sport to coach it," Mrs. Teague said, "Coaching is like any other subject. It's just the other side of education".

Bertha Frank was born September 17, 1901, in Carthage, Missouri. Her family moved to Amity, Arkansas and she lived there until 1923, when she graduated from high school. She married Jesse Teague in 1924, and the couple moved to Oklahoma shortly thereafter.

Mrs. Teague's unlikely career as a coach began in 1927, at the small rural school located six miles north of Ada, in southeastern Oklahoma. Although she had organized a basketball team at Cairo School in Coal County, during her first teaching job, Mrs. Teague had never coached on a competitive level. Nor had she ever played a game of basketball in her life.

Her husband Jess had been hired to teach at Byng. He would later become the school's first superintendent and serve forty years in that position. His wife taught first grade for thirty-nine years. When there was no one else to instruct the girls' basketball team, she was assigned that position, which she held for four decades. Always up to a challenge Mrs. Teague took this job very seriously.

She said, "I got a little book and the first year my girls won a pennant. I was hooked for the next 43 years. What I wanted to do was give the girls something in athletics they could be proud of."

She found that girls' basketball was not as accepted as the boys' programs. In fact, few public schools and even fewer colleges offered athletics for girls. Many people even believed that girls were not physically capable of taking part in contact sports such as basketball. It took years for the public to accept girls playing competitively.

Today, girls' basketball is one of the most popular high school sporting events. Colleges and universities offer scholarships and their teams compete for national honors. Credit for bringing about many of these changes and attitudes has been given to Bertha Teague.

In 1989, when she was inducted into the

Oklahoma Sports Hall of Fame, Mrs. Teague said, "I'm so happy because girls' basketball has not always been accepted. When I started coaching in the 'bloomer days', girls basketball was a PE, backyard game. I'm happy to know the public is accepting the girls' game."

In later years she reflected that her victories and trophies were overshadowed by the pride she felt for the positive changes she made in the sport.

In the beginning, Mrs. Teague's girls wore

Former Governor David Hall, presenting an award to Mrs. Teague. Photo, Courtesy of Omega Johnson.

bloomers and practiced on a dirt court. The first five teams won 100 games and only lost ten. And that was just the beginning!

The 1930's known for the Great Depression were years of accomplishment for the Lady Pirates. During a ten-year span, they won 289 games and lost eight, a winning percentage of .973. Mrs. Teague won eight district, six regional and four state titles during the 1930s. Her teams won 99 games in a row from 1936 through 1939, claiming three straight state championships. Their winning streak was broken in 1939 in the state tournament semifinals.

Former player and later Mrs. Teague's traveling companion, Omega Landrith Johnson was on that losing team. She said, "That was my first year to play and I remember how bad we felt that we lost. Not so much for ourselves but that Mrs. Teague didn't make it to one hundred wins."

If the regular season games only had been counted, and not the tournaments, Byng would have won more than one hundred games in succession

During the 1940's Mrs. Teague's teams went for an entire decade without winning another "big trophy". Still, the girls won 310 games and lost only seven. They took seven district and five regional titles during that decade.

The era of the 1950s brought the development of other good basketball programs across the state. Competition was keener. Nevertheless, the Lady Pirates went on to win three district and three regional crowns, and two state championships. From 1955 to 1957 they won ninety-seven games and lost eight, but they were defeated in the state championship all three years. Their record for the decade was 288 wins and 38 losses.

The 1960s were phenomenal years for the Lady Pirates. They would be Mrs. Teague's last years to coach. The 1965 team went undefeated one of five of Mrs. Teague's team to reach that goal. Two other of Mrs. Teague's teams lost only once and her final team lost only twice. In her last game in the state finals, the lady pirates captured the Class A state championship.

Mrs. Teague's legendary coaching career ended in a storybook fashion. The team never led in the entire game and won on a last second desperation shot in the state finals.

Playing on the 1965 undefeated team was one of her most outstanding players, Bettie Taylor Estes-Rickner who held almost every scoring record during the mid-sixties. In her senior year, Bettie broke the state scoring record of 49 points and for a while held three state records. She was chosen three times by the Daily Oklahoman to be on their All Tournament Team. A forward and an All-Stater, Bettie is now Executive Director of Libraries and Information Technology Services for the Putnam City School District. She said, "Mrs. Teague was the last person to quit so it was hard for you to quit while you were playing for her."

She added, "She was far more than just a coach. She was my best friend."

Bettie lived several miles from school, and on game days frequently went to the coach's home and ate dinner with Mr. and Mrs. Teague. Just as often, she spent the night at the Teague's home.

Known as a firm taskmaster, Mrs. Teague had definite opinions. During the off seasons, she did not allow her girls to play softball or roller skate, in case they would get hurt. They couldn't leave a game with a boy unless it was for a special occasion, like Valentines Day or a Saturday tournament win, and even then, arrangements had to be made in advance. Many of her former students became basketball coaches. One of Bettie's fellow all-staters, Karen Veith, married the famed Coach Bobby Knight of Indiana University, who went on to establish and maintain a basketball dynasty. He now coaches at Texas Tech.

Asked by other coaches for advice, and willing to share her expertise, Mrs. Teague authored the book that many consider to be the bible of girls basketball, *Basketball for Girls,* published in 1962 by Ronald Press. Reprinted three times, the book has been placed in libraries and on many coaches shelves as a reference.

In explaining her concept of the book, Mrs. Teague said, "At that time, we didn't have that many clinics for girls. There was a real need for the fundamental instruction it gives. I had a girl write to me from New York State to say they had followed the fundamentals given in my book and won two championships with them. You couldn't ask for a better review than that".

In *Basketball for Girls,* Mrs. Teague writes, "There are a few simple things that the coach can put into practice that will head off trouble and keep team morale at a higher plane during the playing season. These rules can be put into use at the beginning of the season. Boys and girls traveling on the same bus to games should be seated separate, the boys on one side of the bus and the girls on the opposite side. The players should not be permitted to date on game nights. They should be required to leave off smoking. If the player does not like the game well enough to keep these simple rules, she is a poor risk for a member of the team."

Through the years, generations of the same family played for Mrs. Teague. Bettie's mother was an All-Stater in the 1940s. Bettie remembers Mrs. Teague as being a lady; always well dressed, carrying a pouch containing her dress shoes. Not only was she a lady herself, she demanded the same from her players. They were expected to dress like ladies, no pants on game days. "In fact, game days were special, the day we wore our best clothes," she said.

In the many newspaper articles printed about the Teague dynasty, she was always referred to as Mrs. Teague, not Teague or even Coach Teague. Bettie remembers, as a teenager, going to a sports banquet and being upset because the speaker, Governor David Hall referred to Jess and Bertha. To the townspeople they were Mr. and Mrs. Teague.

Mrs. Teague's life, as a basketball coach, involved more than winning games. From the beginning, she realized that young country girls needed something more than school. They must establish and accomplish goals, and feel the pride of achievements. They needed a sport like their male counterpart's. Basketball was the answer. This was in the 1920's and 1930's long before the women's liberation movement.

A dedicated Mrs. Teague was always looking for ways to better the game. One of her changes was the dress of the players. In the early 1930's she did away with the bloomers and designed maroon satin pants with gold satin tops. The outfit was one piece because she hated someone having their shirt tale out. The sleeveless blouse had a knit band around the waist to give it a fitted appearance and still permit freedom. The shorts had an elastic inset to keep them from riding up. The Byng girls basketball team were the first in Oklahoma and likely the first in the nation to wear shorts. Mrs. Teague was proud of the uniforms she designed, "My girls were the best-looking on the court".

Omega Johnson said, "Few people knew that Mrs. Teague's degree from OSU was in costume design and art. She also pioneered the use of knee pads, long socks, and high-top tennis shoes."

Mrs. Teague helped establish the Oklahoma High School Girls Basketball Coaches Association in 1962 and served as president for seven years. She resigned the office in 1969, when she retired from active coaching. She was named the association's permanent "Ambassador of Good Will" and continued to be active in the organization.

She organized and conducted the first girls basketball clinic/camp in southwestern United States. She also led clinics in Oklahoma, Arkansas, Texas, Iowa, Louisiana, and Oregon. Mrs. Teague played lead roles in the creation of the girls All State games (1964), the All-Decade selections (1974), and the Mid-America Tournament (1975).

No sports hall of fame seems complete without mention of Mrs. Teague. She was named National Basketball Committee Coach of the Year in1966, Oklahoma Girls Basketball Coach of the Year in 1969. She was presented the Special Service Award by the Oklahoma Men's Coaches Association in 1970, the only woman so honored.

She also received the Coach of the Decade three times, (1930s, 1940s, and 1960s) given by the Jim Thorpe Athletic Awards Committee.

In announcing Mrs. Teague's selection to the Hall of Fame for the National Federation of State High Schools Associations, the committee called her, "the most influential coaching figure in girls' high school basketball history and the most celebrated female in Oklahoma sports history. In addition to her innovative and successful coaching skills, she emerged as a national figure in the growth of both her sport and girls sports in general".

Retirement and even the 1981 death of her number one supporter, husband Jess, didn't slow her

---

down.. She toured the country as a speaker and clinician, usually driven by her good friend and former player Omega. An all-state sophomore for Mrs. Teague in 1939, Omega made sure Mrs. Teague never missed any All State games, state tournaments, or other girls basketball functions. Omega accompanied her all over the country to accept the many prestigious awards she was given. She said Mrs. Teague was a great traveling companion, and never criticized her driving. Omega said she was always a lady. In later years she did relent and sometimes wore pants.

The two of them were major organizers of the annual holiday tournament, the Bertha Teague Mid-America Classic. This event has grown into one of the most prestigious regular season tournaments of its kind drawing the top girls' basketball programs in Oklahoma as well as other states.

Mrs. Teague broke the barrier against women in 1971, when she was the only female inducted into the Oklahoma Athletic Hall of Fame. In 1983, she was the first woman inducted into the National Federation of State High Schools Hall of Fame. In 1985, she was received into the Oklahoma Women's Hall of fame and in 1989, along with rodeo great Jim Shoulders and football hero Billy Vessels, she was inducted into the Oklahoma Sports Hall of Fame.

The ultimate honor in basketball was given her in 1985, when the Boston Celtics of the National Basketball Association nominated her for the Naismith Hall of Fame, making her the first woman considered for enshrinement. Bill McKray, Information Director of the Boston Celtics said, " ...her reputation is such, nationally, that in discussion of high school girls' basketball, one inevitably gets around to Bertha Frank Teague and her superb record."

Upon her induction into the Oklahoma Commission on the Status of Women she received the following letter

The White House

April 5, 1985

Dear Mrs. Teague,

I was proud to learn of your many contributions to womens basketball. You can take great pride in your achievements. Stories like yours are encouraging and inspiring, for it is hardworking, dedicated individuals like you who make this Nation great. Nancy joins with me in sending our warm best wishes for every future success.

Sincerely,

Ronald Reagan

Mrs. Teague was honored by three Oklahoma governors, Bartlett, Hall and Nigh. Governor Nigh cited her contributions in a proclamation from the Governor's office on April 25, 1982. He commended Mrs. Teague for her incomparable accomplishments as well as her ongoing services to the world of sports."

Mr. and Mrs. Teague had one daughter, Geneva Billey who lives in the Oklahoma City area. Mrs. Teague found time to be active in her church, The First Baptist Church in Ada, and other professional and social organizations.

In 1991, when the Women's Basketball Hall of Fame opened in Knoxville, Tennessee, Mrs. Teague was one of the class of 25 inaugural Hall of

Famers inducted. This time Omega accepted the trophy for her, as her friend had died that June, at the age of ninety-two.

Delivering the eulogy at the packed funeral service was former student and friend Bettie Taylor Estes-Rickner, who said, "The person she was, cannot exclude basketball or athletics in general, but to us, she was much more. The depth of her influence will live on years after this day when we honor her life a last time."

At the close of her speech Bettie asked people to stand: first everyone who played for Mrs. Teague, then everyone who had been her student, followed by coaching colleagues, fellow teachers, and parent of a child or patron of the Byng community. She closed with anyone who was an admirer, acquaintance or family friend – there was not an empty seat!

The Teague Log

1,157-115 career record
8 state championships
22 state tournament appearances
22 regional titles
27 district titles
38 conference titles
5 unbeaten seasons
98 game winning streak
Named coach of the year in 1967 and 1969
Named coach of the decade in 1974

Kay Starr

The Wheel of Fortune Keeps Spinning Around

Kay Starr is regarded as one of the great voices of the "Big Band Era." At thirteen she had her own radio show. At fifteen she sang with the Glenn Miller Orchestra. Still performing at age 71, she toured the United Kingdom with Pat Boone. One of Oklahoma's most famous singers of the 1950s is still going strong.

The train slowed at the small town water tower not making a complete stop. The note pinned on the tiny girl, asleep in the passenger car, said to drop her off at Dougherty, Oklahoma. The conductor carried her to the door and handed her to a man waiting at the track. Three- year old Kathryn La Verne Starks' mother had put her on the train in Dallas, Texas, and the child woke in her grandparent's home in Oklahoma.

This was one of the earliest and most precious memories of singer Kay Starr. Summertime visits to Dougherty were an important part of her life. Although she moved away when she was three years old, she always called Oklahoma home.

Born on July 21, 1922, in Davis, her father, Harry Starks was a full-blooded Iroquis Indian, and her mother Annie was mixed American Indian and Irish. The family moved to Dallas in 1925. There, her father found work installing sprinkler systems.

During the depression years, finances were

tight, and Mrs. Starks raised chickens in a hen house in the back yard. It was here that Kay began singing at the age of nine. After school she gave concerts to the chickens as they sat on their roosts. Kay said this was the best audience she ever had, as they did not boo or shout out requests.

While her parents thought this was amusing, her aunt Nora recognized her talent and suggested her mother enter her in local radio station WWR-Dallas' weekly talent contest.

Kay was nervous about singing, but this debut also entailed a yoyo contest. Kay loved to yoyo, and she swung the string as she sang, " Potatoes are cheaper, Tomatoes are cheaper." Then, while performing the "around the world" trick, she sang, "Now is the Time to Fall in Love". That day, at Dallas's Melba Theater, Kay won over the other contestants and kept retuning and winning for several weeks. Eventually, the station retired her by giving Kay her own three- times-weekly, fifteen-minute radio program. She sang pop tunes and hillbilly music earning three dollars a night and a bundle of fan mail.

Three months later her father was transferred to Memphis, Tennessee. Kay soon landed her own show, *Starr Time* on WREC in Memphis, along with being a featured singer on the station's popular *Saturday Night Jamboree* program. Kay was known as "the kid" and whenever a song was requested, the master of ceremonies would say, "Aw, let the kid do it."

Because of constant misspellings in fan letters and publicity, Kathryn Starks changed her name to Kay Starr.

Kay's first big break came in 1937 when bandleader/violinist Joe Venuti came to Memphis to play at the Peabody Hotel. His contract required his band to have a girl singer, which they did not.

After hearing Kay on the radio, he and his road manager went to her home to discuss hiring her with her parents. They agreed and following their three - week engagement at the Peabody Hotel, Venuti, impressed with Kay, hired her to sing with the band each summer for the next two years.

Because she was only fifteen, Kay's mother

Kay Star. Photo courtesy of Kay Starr.

traveled with her. The young star and her mother were always close, "Like two nuts in a shell," Kay said.

"We never told anyone how old I was. We let on like we were sisters."

Kay said they bought clothes to make her look older at Salvation Army thrift stores. She claims she ruined her feet by wearing high heeled shoes at such an early age. That probably led to the two hip replacements she had later in life.

Joe Venuti, in an attempt to further Kay's career pitched her talents to Gil Rodin, manager of Bob Crosby's Orchestra. Crosby needed a female vocalist for his 1939 upcoming appearances on the *Camel Caravan* radio program. Kay landed the job. She and her mother traveled to New York where she made her network radio debut singing "Memphis Blues". However, after two weeks, the management decided they needed a more seasoned performer.

Within a few days, Kay received an offer from the most famous band in the land. She was hired to sing with the Glenn Miller Orchestra to replace an ailing Marion Hutton. During her two-week stint with the legendary band she made her first recordings on the Bluebird label, singing "Love with A Capitol YOU" and "Baby Me".

Still in high school, Kay returned to Memphis where she graduated with the class of 1940. She then moved to California and resumed working with Joe Venuti, until the general draft call in World War II caused the break up of the band.

She briefly sang with Wingy Manone's New Orleans Jazz Band. Then in 1943, she replaced Lena Horne with the Charlie Barnett Orchestra. During this time she recorded on the Decca label. Unfortunately, her association with the Barnett Orchestra ended abruptly in 1945, when Kay caught pneumonia and collapsed during an Army camp show. When she recovered, she realized she had lost her voice.

Rather than risk a surgery that might have altered her singing style, she treated her vocal cords and refrained from speaking and singing for six months. She returned with a deeper and huskier voice that has since become her trademark.

Her solo career was launched in Los Angeles at Hollywood's "Streets of Paris" and other nightclubs. Capitol Records then signed her to a contract in 1947 and invited her to sing two songs as part of their all star *Volumes of Jazz* series. Capitol Record's large roster of female talent included Peggy Lee, Ella Mae Morse, Jo Stafford, and Margaret Whiting.

Kay said, "In those days you had to be able to sing all kinds of music as there was a lot of competition— but no one else sang country."

Her first top ten hit came in 1949 with "So Tired" followed by "Hoop-Dee-Doo" which charted at number 2.

Back in Dougherty, on a hometown visit, Kay heard a jukebox recording of Pee Wee King's fiddle tune, "Bonaparte's Retreat" and fell in love with the melody. She received permission from Roy Acuff's publishing house to record the song, which became her first major hit and sold almost one million copies.

Kay recorded several other songs in the county genre including successful duets with "Tennessee" Ernie Ford. In an interview, Kay said, "I loved Ernie Ford. The first time we sang together, I went to the recording studio to try out. He sang eight bars, then I sang eight bars and we looked at each other and knew we were right together. We were friends until the day he died."

On January 17, 1952, Kay was awakened and

called into Capitol's Melrose studios late one night, to record a rush release of a new song titled "Wheel of Fortune". Kay's version was released along with two others on competing labels in February of 1952, and immediately became a big success. Ultimately becoming the song most associated with Kay Starr and her biggest hit, "Wheel of Fortune" earned Kay her first gold record and went on to become the number two top selling single of 1952. Remaining on the charts as number one for ten weeks this became Kay's signature song.

From 1948 to 1954, she charted 27 hits with Capitol. She demonstrated her versatility by recording a number of hits in varying genres, earning her the title of "hit maker" whether it be jazz, country, pop, spiritual, Broadway tunes, or rhythm and blues.

In 1955, she moved her contract from Capitol to RCA Records. Shortly thereafter, she hit both American and British charts with her million selling gold record "Rock and Roll Waltz". The song went on to become the number two best selling single of 1956 in the United States and the number one single of the year on the United Kingdom charts. This earned Kay the distinction of being the first female vocalist with a top hit in the "rock and roll" era.

She recorded several jazz albums including *Loser Weepers* and *I Cry by Night* and a county album titled *Just Plain Country*. She toured in concerts across the United States and England and performed at the Sands, Riviera, and Fremont Hotels in Las Vegas and Harrah's in Reno, Nevada. She also performed on stage, television and movies.

Kay cut back on her performances in the 1970's to devote more time to her family. She moved her mother from Oklahoma to her home in California.

She was featured in the revue *3 Girls* with Helen O'Connell and Margaret Whiting. In 1993, she toured the United Kingdom as part of Pat Boone's *April Love* Tour. Her first "live" album *Live At Freddy's* was released in 1997.

Kay loves retirement. "I had a wonderful career for over thirty years. When you love what you are doing, it is exciting to wake up each day. I have wonderful memories and I keep in contact with many friends like Pat Boone, Roy Clark, Chet Atkins, the Blackwood brothers and Oklahoma friends such as Charles and Geneva Sarratt".

Her daughter and grandson live close by in California. Kay is single and said she had been married too many times to count.

In all her years of show business, she never had the opportunity to meet another Oklahoma singer, Patti Page. In 2006, she attended a performance in Los Angeles. She enjoyed the show and meeting Patti Page, whom, she said, was charming.

Kay visits Oklahoma as often as possible. Both her parents are buried at the cemetery on the Kay Starr Trail in Dougherty. The trail was named for her by the Oklahoma House of Representatives when they named June 17, 1995, as Kay Starr Day. She cut the ribbon for the trail and served as honorary parade marshall in the town of Sulphur.

Governor David Boren had presented her with an "Outstanding Oklahoman" Award in 1976. She was inducted into the Oklahoma Hall of Fame in the fall of 1988 and the Oklahoma Music Hall of Fame in 2002.

In honor of Kay, there is a star for the Starr on the Hollywood Walk of Fame.

Jeane Kirkpatrick, Ambassador to the United Nations,
Photo, Courtesy of The Oklahoma Heritage Association.

Jeane Jordan Kirkpatrick

United States Ambassador to the United Nations

President Reagan called her "a giant among the diplomats of the world." As a scholar, political scientist, historian, and advocate for America's foreign policy, Dr. Jeane Kirkpatrick is one of the modern world's experts on geopolitical issues. She served as the United States Ambassador to the United Nations from 1980 to 1984 and was awarded the Medal of Freedom, our nation's highest civilian honor.

Sitting in the foyer of Dr. Kirkpatrick's office at the American Enterprise Institute in Washington D.C., I was more than a little nervous. I was about to interview the woman who has often been referred to as one of the most intelligent woman in the world.

The door opened and a small lady, in a blue pantsuit, carrying a deli sandwich walked in. She grinned and held out her hand, "You must be my visitor from Oklahoma. I hope you don't mind if I eat lunch while we visit."

I relaxed. I immediately liked this political legend from Oklahoma and knew this was going to be a delightful visit.

She escorted me into her office where a window overlooked the Washington Monument and the city she calls home. She said, "I like to stand here and look out early in the morning. The view is of the Jefferson Memorial and the Washington Mall. On mornings when the humidity is low you can see to the Potomac River and the Virginia shore. Sometimes I watch the morning traffic as people make their way to work and now and then there is a sailboat on the river."

Behind her desk, books fill the floor to ceiling shelves. Around the room are Oklahoma mementos, including a picture of her being inducted into the Oklahoma Hall of Fame. She said her father was more impressed with her receiving that award than anything else she ever accomplished. On a nearby table sat a sculpture of Will Rogers presented to her by former Oklahoma Congressman Mickey Edwards. Dr Kirkpatrick pointed to a replica of the famous James Earle Fraser sculpture, "The End of The Trail" given to her by an Indian friend, C. M. Matsun. He gave the statue to her to be placed at the United Nations, saying she would find an appropriate place for it. It was put in an inside courtyard at the U.N.

In the next hour, I discovered that one of the most respected women in the world is also warm, coy, feisty, and fun.

She has fond memories of growing up in Oklahoma. Thinking of her early years, she said, "I had a wonderful Oklahoma childhood. My family imbued me with the frontier spirit. It is a can-do spirit...the frontier ethic that you can do anything—everything—always. This is what I heard, 'Jeane, you can do that.' I was always told doing something well is just a matter of trying harder."

A third generation Oklahoman, her grandfather and grandmother eloped to Oklahoma from

Texas. They settled and farmed in what was then Indian Territory.

Jeane Duane Jordan was born on November 19, 1926, in Duncan, to Welcher and Leona Jordan. Eight years later her only brother Jerry was born. Her father was a drilling contractor and his wife was his bookkeeper. They lived next door to the CEO of Halliburton, a major oil company based in Oklahoma.

A homemaker and an accountant, her mother, Leona, had wanted to attend college. When her family's cotton crop was destroyed, she settled for business school in Ft. Worth. There, she met Welcher. They were married, moved to Durant, and later to Duncan in southwestern Oklahoma.

Childhood friend Buddy Campbell still lives in Duncan. He remembers their walking to Emerson School together in the first grade. "At that time Jeane went by her middle name, Duane. The teacher said she had to go by her first name. That was when she became Jeane."

Buddy still has a copy of the school newspaper, which reads, "The Emerson Gazette Club met Thursday, Feb, 29, 1936. The secretary announced the program, which was a reading by Duane Jordan titled *George Washington*." She was already showing an interest in history, government and public speaking. At the age of ten she spent her birthday money on a thesaurus.

Her earliest memories include living in the tornado belt, amid dust storms and red dirt. She still remembers her father outside studying storm clouds with his neighbor.

Speaking at the Duncan bicentennial in September 1987, Jeane said, "I had enormous encouragement in Emerson School, from my teacher, from my friends, from my parents, of course, but especially from those teachers in Emerson School who not only set standards for us but high standards—and really kept us at it until we met them."

The most important person in her life was her mother, whose motto was, "He or She who thinks he or she can –can."

"She did not live to see me become Ambassador, which I have always deeply regretted," Jeane said.

"Mother made sure I had speech lessons from the time I was three years old. I was the youngest child in the neighborhood and didn't like it that I couldn't go to school. At that time there were no schools for three year olds. I apparently liked the speech classes very much and no doubt they were very useful."

Since then she has been praised as a dynamic speaker who thinks fast on her feet.

Her mother wanted the best education and preparation for life for her children. When Jeane was twelve years old the family moved to Mt. Vernon, Illinois, which her mother called "An All American City".

Jeane Jordan, who was editor of the high school paper and star of her senior play, graduated in 1944, and enrolled in Stephens College, Columbia, Missouri. In 1946, she received a bachelor's degree in political science from Barnard College in New York, and in 1950, she was awarded a masters degree from Columbia University in New York City.

From 1950 to 1952, she worked as a research analyst for her future husband, Evron Kirkpatrick, at the office of intelligence research at the U.S. State Department.

However, she did not like working in a big bureaucracy. An opportunity arose for her to study at the Institute de Science Politique in Paris. She received a scholarship from the French Government very much like the Fulbright in the United States. This was an important experience for her, an opportunity to travel, and to improve her French.

Evron and Jeane were married in 1955. He was her mentor and fifteen years her senior. For the next few years, she delayed her career to raise three sons, Douglas, John, and Stuart.

She is quoted in *Contemporary Authors* as saying, "My experiences demonstrate to my satisfaction that it is both possible and feasible for women in our times to successfully combine traditional and professional roles, that it is not necessary to ape men's career patterns—starting early and keeping one's nose to the grindstone, but that, instead, one can do quite different things at different stages of one's life. All that is required is a little luck and a lot of work."

She joined the faculty of Georgetown University in 1967, and became a full professor of political science the next year. In 1968, she finished her Ph.D. at Columbia University, writing her dissertation on Peron's Argentina. She became Leavey Professor of Political Science at Georgetown in 1978.

In the 1970's, Dr. Kirkpatrick became involved in politics as a democrat, and was active in the campaigns of former Vice-President and presidential candidate Hubert Humphrey. Later, she became disillusioned with the Democratic Party and published a number of articles in political science journals criticizing the foreign policy of President Jimmy Carter.

This criticism brought her to the attention of Republican presidential candidate Ronald Reagan. She met with Reagan and each was favorably impressed with the other. He hired her as a foreign policy adviser during his successful 1980 campaign. Upon winning the election, Reagan appointed Dr. Kirkpatrick to serve as the United States Ambassador to the United Nations, a position she held for four years. She became the first woman ever to head the U.S. delegation to the United Nations and was the only woman chief delegate among the 157 nations. Women represented smaller countries as Egypt, Ghana, and Liberia, but she was the only representative from a major country.

Dr. Kirkpatrick said the men in the United Nations were shocked and did not appreciate her heading the human rights delegation. Her ten to fifteen years in a university experience made it easy for her to speak before a group.

"I was the first woman on the National Security Council, and they made it clear they didn't think that was an appropriate place for me."

Dr. Kirkpatrick also became the first woman member of the Reagan cabinet and, for two years remained the only one. She also served as a member of Reagan's national security team. "I was the only woman in our history, I think, who has sat in regularly at top level foreign policy meetings.

"These arenas have always been closed to women, not only here but in most countries. It is terribly important to the future of the world for women to take part in making decisions that shape our destiny."

She admitted that sexism is rampant in the United Nations and in the U.S. government.

As ambassador, Dr. Kirkpatrick gained international attention through her strong projection of U.S. causes. An ardent anticommunist, she is famous for her "Kirkpatrick Doctrine," which advocates U.S. support of anticommunist governments around the world.

She was praised for being coherent, articulate, firm, honest, and a great communicator. Critics claimed she was dogmatic with an abrasive style. Former Attorney General Ed Meese said she was aggressive but definitely not abrasive. In an interview published in *The Saturday Evening Post,* Meese said President Reagan appreciated Dr Kirkpatrick's directness.

Her resignation as ambassador to the United Nations was submitted to the President to be effective in March of 1985. Much speculation arose as to why she resigned. She said, "The news media cannot bear for anyone to have a personal life."

Dr. Kirkpatrick's husband was very ill with cancer and she felt that she needed to leave New York. She never spoke about that, not wanting her husband to feel responsible for her giving up that position. She felt like she was needed at home to care for him. He died in 1995, and she is happy she had more time to share with him.

When she left the U.N., Dr. Kirkpatrick had become disillusioned with international organizations, especially the United Nations. "As I watched the behavior of the nations of the U.N. (including our own), I found no reasonable ground to expect any one of those governments to transcend permanently their own national interests for those of another country... I conclude that it is a fundamental mistake to think that salvation, justice, or virtue comes through merely human institutions... Democracy not only requires equality but also an unshakable conviction in the value of each person, who is then equal. Cross cultural experience teaches us not simply that people have different beliefs, but that people seek meaning and understand themselves in some sense as members of a cosmos ruled by God."

She also said of the United Nations, "We must belong. We must actively seek to expand the reach of the U.N. I learned that the influence the United States doesn't use in the U.N., France will use. Russia and China are both opposed to us."

The former ambassador is proud of her tenure. "If I do say so myself, I did a very good job."

In 1985, this former democrat, who served the Republicans, officially joined the Republican Party. She believes party membership does not seem to be as important to the younger generation. "My three sons have never had strong political loyalties.

"I am avidly interested in politics. I wouldn't miss watching a convention or a debate. I don't mind making a public statement that I support George Bush."

Frequently mentioned as a presidential candidate or a vice-presidential running mate to George Walker Bush, she has never had any desire to go that route. "Politics," she said, "is a very rough game."

Dr. Kirkpatrick returned to teaching at Georgetown University while serving as chief foreign policy adviser to Senate Republicans. She also served as a member of the President's Foreign Defense Policy Review Board from 1985 to1990; the Defense Policy Review Board from 1985 to 1992; and chaired the Secretary of Defense Commission of Failsafe and Risk Reduction from 1991 to 1992.

She became a fellow at the American Enterprise Institute, a conservative think tank, and wrote a syndicated column and several articles and books. In 1993 she co-founded Empower America, a conservative, public-policy organization. She is also on the board of the National Association of Scholars.

Published works include: *The Regan Phenomenon; Dictatorships and Double Standards: Rationalism and Reason in Politics; The Withering Away of the Totalitarian State; Dismantling the Parties: Reflections of Party Reform.; Party Decomposition; The New Presi-*

dential Elite; Political Women; and *Good Intentions.*

For her brilliant and consistent service as America's international policy advisor, Dr. Kirkpatrick was granted the Medal of Freedom, our nation's highest civilian honor. She has also received presidential medals from the Czech Republic, Hungary, and Israel. She was the recipient of the Gold Medal of the Veterans of Foreign Wars; the Hubert Humphrey Award of the American Political Science Association; The Christian A. Herter Award of the Boston World Affairs Association; the Morgenthau Award of the American Council on Foreign Policy; the Humanitarian Award of B'nai B'rith; the Defender of Jerusalem Award; and honorary degrees from more than a dozen universities.

After her husband died in 1995 she left her position at Georgetown to spend more time reading and writing. She is now with Brookings Institute, a political think tank for economists, sociologists, political scientists, and people who make public policy.

Dr. Jeane Kirkpatrick continues to shape national foreign policy on a multitude of issues such as trade, defense, and the international projection of democracy. She testifies yearly before committees of the Senate and the House of Representatives on national and international defense policy, focusing on matters of utmost importance to our national security.

Mazola McKerson, Mayor of Ardmore, Photo, Courtesy of
The Daily Oklahoman.

Mazola McKerson

Born to Serve

Mazola McKerson was born to serve. As a child, she was a maid to one of Ardmore, Oklahoma's richest families. As an adult she owned one of the most successful restaurants in southeastern Oklahoma and catered parties to the rich and the famous. At 53, she became the Mayor of Ardmore and the first African American female mayor in the United States in a predominately white town with a population of 30,000 or more residents.

Mazola McKerson leaned back on the deck chair. She was enjoying her first Caribbean cruise, the sea breeze on her face. She jumped when she heard the announcement through the ship's sound system, "The Captain would like to invite Mazola McKerson, Mayor of Ardmore, Oklahoma to join him at his table for dinner tonight." She turned to the delighted faces of her fellow travelers and muttered, "Well, I'll be."

Later dressed for dinner, Mazola entered the dining room. At the Captain's table each person had their own waiter and at each place were nine pieces of silverware. She held back a chuckle, as she thought, "And I know exactly what to do with each fork and spoon. My early training as a maid to one of the richest families in Ardmore was good training for this very day."

Mazola had started out as a servant and, now,

she was the only black woman mayor in a predominately white city in the United States. She was still serving. But, now, she was a public servant!

In 1980, on a cruise with other members of Ardmore's City Council she realized how far she had come.

Mazola McKerson was born in Bluff, Oklahoma, a small town 18 miles southeast of Hugo. Her father died when she was very young. Her mother remarried, began a new family, and was unable to care for all 11 children. Mazola went to live with an aunt. She said, "In 1929, when I was nine years old, my aunt took me with her to Ardmore. She did housework and some odd jobs, then she landed a job with Miss Marie Smith and we moved into the servant's quarters.

My aunt Pearl was the cook, and after school I helped cook and set the table for dinner. Even if it was only Miss Marie and her brother, Charlie, the table was set formally with a glass mirror in the center, fresh flowers, and cloth napkins. I remember they always started dinner with tomato juice and caviar on toast points."

"Miss Marie never had any children, and she took me to raise. She bought me clothes and taught me how to answer the telephone and welcome guests and escort them to the drawing room. The butler took me to school as there was not a bus for the colored children."

When Mazola's was in the eleventh grade her aunt became ill, so Mazola dropped out of school and assumed the cooking duties. Miss Marie and Mr. Charlie Smith paid the hospital bills for Aunt Pearl and let Mazola and her aunt continue to live there.

At a church function, Mazola met the best looking man she had ever seen. A former football player, Alfred McKerson was big and robust. Mazola knew immediately this was the man she would marry.

In 1938, Mazola and Alfred were married. They had a small house downtown, three young children and another on the way when her husband joined the service. To bring in extra money, she began making pies and sold chickens, and hams from the house. She bought and raised 50 Rhode Island Reds and some pigs.

In 1942, Maureen Riesen, whose father owned the *Ardmorite,* asked her to prepare a special Sunday dinner. At the end of the delicious meal, she suggested Mazola start a catering service. At the time, Mazola didn't know what the word catering meant and asked the lady to explain. After their conversation Riesen, offered to run a 30-day advertisement in the newspaper for Mazola in order to help her get a business started. After the 30 days lapsed, Mazola had more business than she could handle from her own family kitchen.

"Then I made a deal with the Altrusa Service Club to go in and cook Sunday dinner. We soon outgrew that place. People said, 'why don't you open your own restaurant?' Alfred was home from the service by then and with our savings of $1,300 we came to Curtis Restaurant and Supply in Oklahoma City and bought chairs and tables."

Mazola's Gourmet and Catering Service opened in August 1962. "The first Sunday when I looked out and saw how many people were waiting, I almost went out the back door. We only had 80 chairs. I just rolled up my sleeves and went back to the kitchen. Three hundred people were served that day. I had to keep sending someone to the grocery store for more food."

The Gourmet was open seven days a week,

10: 00 a.m. to 10:00 p.m. The four McKerson children grew up working at the restaurant after school, and her husband helped with the catering business in the hours after his job at Oklahoma Natural Gas Co.

For bridge clubs, receptions, and group functions, a party room was added to the restaurant in 1965. In September 1997, the restaurant was sold, but it never did the same business as when Mazola was in charge.

Those were the days of the oil boom. That time was often called "the Cadillac Days" because many deals were signed on the hood of a Cadillac in the middle of an oil patch. Ardmore was at its height. Oil men, scientists, geologists, and politicians came from everywhere.

Lloyd Noble was a prominent oil producer and philanthropist. He was known as one of the largest drilling contractors in the world and was chairman and president of several oil companies. He was also the founder of the Samuel Roberts Noble Foundation.

Mazola catered dinners at the Noble's 'big house' in town and barbecues, fish fries, and picnics at their cabin north of town. She met many celebrities at the Nobles. Lorne Green, who played Ben Cartwright liked to help with the cooking. John Wayne asked for her recipe for chile con queso.

On February 14, 1950 at 6:00 a.m., Mazola was awakened by a telephone call telling her to come to the big house. Lloyd Noble, at fifty-three years old had died of a sudden heart attack. Mazola spent days preparing food for people who came from around the world to pay their respects.

Mazola faced, on occasion, the prejudice towards blacks that was prevalent in the 40's, 50's and 60's. Although she owned *The Gourmet* she could not eat in her own dining room. The black employees worked in the kitchen, and white employees worked out front.

Mazola said, "I remember, one time, a young serviceman had us do his wedding rehearsal dinner. His mother, who was from Mississippi, asked to meet the person who was in charge, so she could thank her and pay her. When I came out, the mother said loudly, 'Why didn't you tell me this was a nigger place?'"

The woman paid her. When Mazola brought back the change, the groom's mother exclaimed, "This one can count!" It was embarrassing to Mazola but even more so to the young man who had hired her.

The Nobles often flew the McKerson family to Lennox Square in Atlanta to cater receptions. When the flight stopped in Jackson, Mississippi, Mazola and the children had to go outside to the back window of the airport to order lunch.

The restaurant business eventually led to Mazola running for political office. She enjoyed talking politics with her patrons. She was active in the Parent Teacher Association and other school activities. For thirty years she was president of the Ladies of Action, an east side ladies club. The club began giving $25 college scholarships to girls. For several years, now, the club has given $500 scholarships to four students, both boys and girls.

A customer asked if she would run for Ward 4 on Ardmore's city council. Mazola was concerned about the funding, but the customer told her not to worry. He was right. Her supporters raised more than enough. Five other candidates, all men, ran against her. She received as much criticism for being a woman as for being black.

Mazola was elected Ardmore's first black and

first female City Commissioner in 1977. Then, she became Mayor in 1979. At 53 years old she became the first black woman mayor in America for a city of 30,000 or more population. Other black women had served as mayors but were in all black towns. During her six years on the Commission, the city erected a new water treatment plant, public works complex, and fire station. The city hall and police departments were remodeled.

One of former Governor George Nigh's favorite stories is about the time during his first term when he was invited to Ardmore for a celebration of Mazola McKerson the city's first black and first woman mayor. The governor asked her if she had encountered any obvious discrimination as mayor. "Oh, yes." She replied. "There are some people who still think a woman shouldn't be mayor."

She was appointed by Governor George Nigh to the Governor's Commission on the Status of Women, and served as chairman. For three years, she represented Ardmore on the Oklahoma Municipal League Board.

Mazola is proud to be a trustee of Ardmore's Higher Education Center. She is the oldest member of the board both in age and longevity. She has served sixteen years.

More than thirty years ago, she was asked to cook the Passover dinner for the Jewish community in the Ardmore area. It would take her several days but she enjoyed this and continued even after retiring from many other activities. However, in 2003, the temple discontinued the dinner as membership had dwindled.

In 1984, Mazola was the recipient of the Woman of the Year Award at the Pioneer Woman Museum in Ponca City. On September 5th, Governor George Nigh presented the awards to other nominees Hannah Atkins, June Brooks and Ruby Hall. Unfortunately Mazola was unable to attend because of the death of her daughter two days before the ceremony. The award was later presented to her in a special ceremony in Stillwater.

In 1997, the Oklahoma Commission on the Status of Women inducted Mazola into the Oklahoma Women's Hall of Fame. Others honored that year were Dr. Isabel Baker, Norma Eagleton, Dr. Kay Goebel, Ruth Hardman, Beverly Horse, and Senator Penny Williams. The women were honored for being pioneers in their field or project, acting as role models, making a difference in the state or their community and being involved in women's issues, or serving as a public policy advocate for issues important to women. They are women who have exemplified the Oklahoma Spirit.

Mazola believes her biggest accomplishment was raising four children, all with college degrees. Her children never knew there were choices about going to school, church, or college. The only question was where they would go.

The oldest McKerson son, Donald, attended Morehouse, an all men's college in Atlanta, often considered the best black school in the country. He now lives in Atlanta and retired from Time Warner.

Daisy, the oldest daughter, graduated from Luther School in Tacoma, Washington. She served as a city planner and head of Tacoma's Community Development. After her death, a building at Luther was dedicated in her name and the Daisy Marie McKerson Stallworth scholarship for black ladies was formed.

Flossie (now Thurston), went to the Spellman Black School in Atlanta, and is now a program leader in Youth Development at Langston University

The youngest son Alfred received a degree

in math and computer science, and is a sales representative for an automobile dealership in Atlanta. He recently sold over 100 cars and was named the Salesman of the Year for his company.

Mazola also is the proud grandmother of 10 grandchildren and ten great-grandchildren.

In 1983, Ardmore was named a finalist for the "All American City." In the qualification process members of the community traveled to Baltimore to answer questions from a twelve-member panel of judges. Asked how minorities were treated in Ardmore, Mazola stepped to the podium.

"I am happy to say minorities are just plain citizens in Ardmore. Whenever there is a problem we always get involved."

Ardmore was named the "All American City" because of a woman who knew how to serve and dedicated her life to the service of others.

MAZOLA
McKERSON
FOR
CITY COMMISSIONER
WARD 4
Ardmore, Oklahoma

Primary-Tues. Mar. 15, 1977 — Your Vote And Support Appreciated

Doris Eaton Travis

Still Dancing at 102 Years Old

Doris Eaton Travis received a Bachelor of Arts with Distinction degree from the University of Oklahoma at 88 years of age. At 95 she wrote a book about her remarkable life as a dancer with the Ziegfeld Follies and Arthur Murray Studies. The book was published by the University of Oklahoma Press and was a finalist for the Oklahoma Book Award. The day after she received the Distinguished Service Award from the Oklahoma Center for the Book, Mrs. Travis turned 100 years old. Each year she returns to New York City to dance at the Ziegfeld Girls Reunion and the Broadway Cares/Equity Fights Aids Easter Bonnet Event in New York City. At 102, Doris Eaton Travis is still dancing.

The popular song of the day, in 1911, was twenty-three year old Irving Berlin's first big hit, "Alexander's Rag Time Band". As seven year-old Doris Eaton began her career as a professional dancer, she never imagined that by the age of fourteen she would be on the stage with the popular Irving Berlin.

She first appeared with her brothers and sisters in stock company productions in Washington, D.C. and Baltimore. The talented children's long blond curls and big blue eyes caught the attention of producers and opened the doors to stardom. The twenty-year period from 1911 to 1931 was a time of great success for Doris and her siblings, known as "The Eatons of Broadway."

Seven children were born to Charles and Mary Eaton. Five of them became successful in show business. They were often referred to as "The Seven Little Eatons," although the two older children were not performers.

Doris was born on March 4, 1904, in Norfolk, Virginia, where her father was a linotype operator for the newspaper. When Doris was three, to increase his salary, he moved the family to Washington, D.C. A year later, Doris joined her two older sisters, ten-year-old Pearl and seven-year-old Mary, at Miss Cora Shreve's Dancing School.

In the summer of 1912, the road company production of *The Blue Bird*, the previous season's biggest hit on Broadway, came to town. An ad in the *Washington Post* announced auditions to cast twenty to thirty local children.

Doris's oldest sister Evelyn saw the ad and knew, that at seventeen, she was too old to try out but she became excited about the opportunity for her three sisters. Evelyn was always fascinated with the theater, and although, she never performed, she was the one who started the Eatons on their show business careers. Their Mother also was always enamored by the theater. She didn't push her children but she strongly encouraged them and traveled with them throughout their careers.

At the tryouts, Mary and Doris were selected for specific roles and Pearl was chosen as an extra for the group scenes. They danced in eight performances a week for two weeks and were each paid fifty cents a performance. They earned an additional twelve dollars a week for the family. That seemed like a lot of money and it all went into the family pot, from which the girls received a small allowance. For the rest of their lives, this became the practice. Whoever was working contributed to the family pot. From time to time, the primary breadwinner varied.

After *The Blue Bird*, the three sisters and younger brother Joe were hired by the Poli stock companies, in Washington and Baltimore, for several productions over the next three to four years. The local stock company managers knew if they needed three or four or more children, they could call Mama Eaton and hire them all at one place. The gender didn't matter. They could put pants on the girls or dresses on the boys and that worked out fine.

The children became seasoned troopers. For each show, they spent one week in rehearsals, and one week appearing on stage. Between plays, they went home, attended school, took dancing lessons, and practiced on the broken down piano. Soon, they were making more money than their father.

In 1916, an opportunity came for the girls to recreate their roles in *The Bluebird* in New York City. Their mother borrowed $200 from her brother, packed canned foods and her Sterno stove in a trunk, and she and the girls moved to New York. Not yet a city of skyscrapers and traffic, New York was still an adventure. Motor cars moved down the streets along with horseless carriages. Transportation was usually by subway. Taxis had only recently appeared on the streets and were available for fifty cents a mile.

New York City was the theatrical manufacturing center of America. Not only were there such well known Broadway theaters as the Apolla, the Palace, the Ritz, and the New Amsterdam, but traveling shows also usually originated in New York. Road shows were the lifeline for the theaters as there was a huge demand for live entertainment through-out the country. By 1920, over fifty legitimate the-aters operated in the Times Square area and new theatrical productions seemed to open daily.

Soon the rest of the family joined them in New York. The seven Eatons lived in a small flat but some were usually on the road so they were able to man-age in a limited space. New York was an exciting place, and these were thrilling times for the family.

Their father obtained a part-time position working at the *New York World*, first as a linotype operator and then later as a proofreader. He couldn't land a full-time job as it was difficult to find work in those times. Their mother's pursuits were directed toward the children and their budding careers. She made the rounds of the theatrical managers, often sitting for hours in waiting rooms, just to be told to come back the next day. When she wasn't looking for jobs for the children, she was backstage at the theater or on the road with one or more of them. Theatrical managers liked dealing with her and knew that she could be counted on to have her chil-dren well behaved and at the right place at the right time. No one under the age of eighteen traveled without her or older sister Evelyn.

Doris was on the road for most of 1916, tour-ing the eastern United States. For the stock compa-nies they usually traveled by train and stayed in boarding houses or hotels. These shows often lasted two weeks. Touring companies were often one-night stands. The Eatons arrived in town in the morning, performed in the evening, and then boarded another train to the next town that night. Most of Doris's early memories are of traveling.

Doris was determined to complete the eight grade. Because of travel during the school year it was necessary for her to attend summer school. High school was never an option because the week after she completed the eight grade she was on stage appearing in *the Ziegfeld Follies.*

Dancing in the chorus of the Follies was the biggest break in her career. The 1918 show opening at the New Amsterdam Theater starred Eddie Can-

Doris Travis, Star of the Ziegfeld Follies. Courtesy of Doris Eaton Travis.

tor, Will Rogers, W.C. Fields, Lillian Lorraine, Ann Pennington, and Marilyn Miller. At age fourteen, Doris was the youngest performer.

Ziegfeld shows were extravaganzas, (beyond all other Broadway revues and musicals) with scores of dancers, chorus girls and showgirls, brilliant stars, wonderful music, and the best comic talent in the country. Flo Ziegfeld hired the youngest, most beautiful girls on Broadway and dressed them in elegant costumes. Irving Berlin's song, *A Pretty Girl is Like a Melody* became forever identified with *The Ziegfeld Follies*. The 1921 Follies cost $250,000 to produce.

The 1920s were a time of great success for the Eatons, especially Mary. Almost every day an article appeared about her in the newspaper. By the end of the decade, her salary soared from $200 a week to $5,000 a week. It was her turn to support the family. She moved them into an apartment overlooking Central Park. On Sundays the theater was dark and they usually entertained friends including Marilyn Miller, George Gershwin, Oscar Levant, William Hart, Clifton Webb, Fred Astaire, and the Warner Brothers.

Doris and her mother traveled to England, Egypt, and back to California where Doris starred in several movies. The first Eaton to go to Hollywood, she introduced the song, "Singing in the Rain" in the *Hollywood Music Box Review*. She married a producer who died from a heart attack a few months after the wedding. Doris returned to New York.

No one realized that the glory days of show business were about to come to an end. The stock market crash of 1929, the depression that followed, and the popularity of motion pictures had a drastic effect on Broadway. For the first time, the Eatons could not find work. With the stage life and the applause no longer there, they found it hard to cope.

Sisters Mary and Pearl turned to alcohol in an attempt to ease the pain of their lost stardom. Unfortunately, it led to their early demise.

A new career lay in front of her. She met Arthur Murray and applied for a job as instructor at then Murray Dance Studios on 42nd Street. She began as a tap dancing teacher and soon also was teaching ballroom dancing. Two years later, she and another instructor opened a studio in Detroit. This was the first Arthur Murray Studio outside of New York and the beginning of Arthur Murray branch studios. She bought out her partner and before long owned eighteen studios in Michigan. Her brother, Charlie, moved to Detroit to help her with the dance studio. Charlie began a vacation-dance program in Havana. In 1950, Doris began a thirteen- week television show that ran for seven years.

In 1940, Doris broke one of her studio rules that instructors could not date students. She went out with Paul Travis and began an eight- year romance. Finally, she tired of the long relationship and began to hang up the telephone when he called her. He caught on and they were married at the church around the corner from her dance studio. He continued to take lessons and often danced with her on the television show. Through the fifty years they were married they spent many delightful evenings dancing together.

Television and rock and roll in the 1960's began drawing interest away from ballroom dancing. At the same time Paul received a lucrative offer to sell his business in Michigan. He and Doris, both sold their companies, and in 1970 bought an 880 acre ranch outside Norman, Oklahoma. They began breeding and racing quarter horses. Doris learned accounting and took over the bookkeeping for Travis ranch. She now wore blue jeans and boots instead of the lovely evening gowns and business attire of the past. She enjoyed the relaxed life and the friendliness of the horse people. They also were winning races.

Places for ballroom dancing were limited in Oklahoma, but country and western dancing was becoming popular. Doris and Paul thought the Cotton-eyed Joe, the two-step and the line dances looked like fun. So they joined an Arthur Murray Studio and learned the new dance steps. On Friday nights, they usually went to The University Club, at the University of Oklahoma. A country and western band played there and soon Doris and Paul were teaching OU faculty and staff members the dances. They expanded those lessons to tango, rhumba, waltz and other ballroom dances.

Now that they were real "Westerners" they decided to throw a party for their friends. It was a grand gala with their guests performing many of the dances. The evening was so successful they began giving two parties a year: each March, to celebrate their wedding anniversary and Doris' birthday, and in November to celebrate Paul's birthday. Paul attended his ninety-ninth birthday in a wheelchair. Doris intended to have a centennial party for Paul but instead it was a memorial. Paul died at 99 years old on June 24, 2000. This was to have been Doris's last party but she hosted another to celebrate her own centennial.

When Doris sold her Michigan studios she still had two goals in life. One was to graduate from college and the other to write about her famous family. One day she voiced her desire for a college education to her husband. He said, "I have listened to you moan and groan about not having a college degree for too many years. The University is fifteen minutes from this ranch. Now either put up or shut up."

That was all she needed. She procured the General Education Development Test program to achieve high school equivalency status, studied for one year, and in the fall of 1980, she enrolled at the University of Oklahoma. Being a college student was one of the great experiences of her life. Twelve years later, in 1988 she graduated from the University of Oklahoma, with distinction. The oldest graduate, she was a Pi Beta Kappa with a 3.65 average.

In 1998, The Oklahoma Heritage Association named her as its Oklahoma Goodwill Ambassador. She danced onstage, recreating an old vaudeville sister act. Her "sister" partner was Chief Justice of the Oklahoma Supreme Court and member of the Hall of Fame, Alma Wilson.

On to her next goal: Doris began with J.R. Morris writing the story of her family. The *University of Oklahoma Press* published *The Days We Danced: The Story of My Theatrical Family,* in 2003, to rave reviews. Her brother Charlie had moved to Norman and helped her recreate old memories. He died in 2004, a year after publication.

Doris was surprised to have a renovation of her show business career in 1997, sixty years after she had left it, "for good." Five of the original Ziegfeld Follies girls were asked to be guests at the reopening of the New Amsterdam Theater on Forty-Second Street. The Walt Disney Company had purchased and restored the old theater to its original elegance. The ABC television program 20/20 featured the "girls" in a backward look at the Ziegfeld era. As part of the taping, Doris performed a routine. She was the only one of the group that could still dance.

Doris made Broadway history when, the next year, she appeared at the New Amsterdam Theater in a tap dance routine for a benefit for Broadway

Cares/Equity Fights AIDS. She danced the Mandy routine that she had done as understudy to Marilyn Miller in the 1919 Follies. She brought down the house. The standing ovation and clapping continued until she began dancing a routine with the chorus. This was a moment show people spend their whole careers hoping for. What a thrill to accomplish this at ninety-four years old.

She was featured on many local and national television shows, *USA Today, U.S. World and News Report,* ABC's *Good Morning America,* and, *The Today Show* on NBC. She made two appearances on the Rosie O'Donnell Show, once in a dance routine with an all male chorus. She said, "More people saw me dance on the Rosie O'Donnell Show than my entire show business career."

She has returned to New York twice a year since 1997, once for the Ziegfeld Girls Reunion and once to dance in the Easter Bonnet AIDS Benefit. In 2002, she danced the Charleston with Rosie O/Donnell. On her 100th birthday she received a huge birthday cake and a rousing ovation from the audience.

Doris returned to Hollywood in 1999, and at the age of 95 filmed a brief dancing-comedy scene with Jim Carey in the movie, *Man on the Moon,* based on the biography of the late comedian, Andy Kaufman. This was her first motion picture in seventy years. She also appeared on the *Howie Mandel Show* where she taught the host the "Ballin' the Jack."

Doris is a popular guest, not only for her dancing ability but her quick wit and lively personality. Her white hair and sparkling blue eyes give her the appearance of an energetic seventy year old. Strength of character has carried her through the years. She doesn't smoke, or drink, gets plenty of rest, does not overeat, and stays active. She says,

"Remember what Alice in Wonderland said, "She kept running as fast as she could to stay where she was. That is what I do- I run as fast as I can to stay where I am."

She still oversees the ranch, although she no longer raises horses. Now, she leases barns, pasture and corrals.

She has a strong belief in the Christian Scientist Religion and studies it every day. She said, "The teachings have given me the courage, hope, and determination to be the best and most that I am capable of being."

Her next project is to complete the archive room in her spacious home. Bookshelves are crammed with scrapbooks and newspaper clippings of the family's careers. File cabinets hold videos of her television programs in Detroit. Two large worktables in the center of the room hold open scrapbooks showing ongoing work.

Recently, she attended a theater production in Oklahoma City. The announcer took his microphone into the audience interviewing people. Not knowing who she was, he asked her if she would like to sing. "No," she said, "I don't sing. I dance." She did a short routine to the delight of the audience.

At 102, Doris Eaton Travis is still dancing.

Here They Are: Oklahoma's Miss America's

When Jennifer Berry was crowned Miss America January 21, 2006, she joined four other Oklahomans named America's ideal woman: Norma Smallwood in 1926, Jane Jayroe in 1967, Susan Powell in 1981, and Shawntel Smith in 1996. Her victory put Oklahoma in a tie with Pennsylvania in Miss America -producing states—surpassed only by California and Ohio, each with six winners.

Oklahoma's Miss Americas have been not only beautiful, but as representatives of middle America, demonstrated the best of values. They share many similarities.

With the crowning of Jennifer it became obvious that they were distinct personalities with some major differences. Jennifer, from Tulsa, was the first to grow up in a city. The other four were raised in small towns.

Although, the others were all singers with dance and musical theater experience, Jennifer was a classic dancer, performing, for her talent, a ballet en pointe.

Jane Jayroe, Susan Powell, and Shawntel Smith all attended Oklahoma City University, Jennifer studied at the University of Oklahoma.

Kay Alexander, executive director of the Miss Oklahoma pageant said, "All the winners are high achievers, motivated, with good work ethics. They are all from close-knit families who are very supportive and from religious backgrounds. Most of them were drawn to the program for the scholarship monies to fund their schooling. Other than Jane, who was only nineteen, the others were a little older, entered the Miss Oklahoma contest more than once and demonstrated some maturity."

Each girl has her own story.

Norma Smallwood

Miss America 1926

During the Roaring Twenties the five-foot-four, eighteen year old Norma Descygne Smallwood from Bristow won the Miss America title. She was the first Native American to win the crown.

In a Bristow contest, at the tender age of one, Norma won her first pageant when she was named Oklahoma's Most Perfect Baby. As a child she won beauty contests in Missouri, Texas, and Oklahoma. In her first year at the Oklahoma College for Women in Chickasha, she was chosen Most Beautiful Girl. Later that year, Rudolph Valentino named her the best dancer in a Charleston contest in Tulsa. As a college sophomore, the Cherokee woman won the Miss Tulsa Pageant, and shortly thereafter, the Miss America crown.

In September, 1926, in Atlantic City, in a King Neptune theme, she won the bathing suit competition and the evening gown Award. She received a $5,000 gold cup, a vaudeville contract, a $1,000 watch, a $1,000 wardrobe, and a mermaid statue.

During her reign, Norma earned over $100,000, more than either Babe Ruth or the President of the United States.

Norma Smallwood, Miss America 1926. Courtesy of the Pioneer Woman Statue and Museum, Ponca City.

In 1928, she married Thomas Gilcrease, wealthy Tulsa oilman and art collector. The marriage ended in a very public divorce. Later Norma married George Bruce, president of Aladdin Petroleum Corporation in Wichita, Kansas. She died in 1966, shortly before Jane Jayroe was crowned Miss America 1967.

Read more about Norma Smallwood in *Petticoats, Politics and Pirouettes, Oklahoma Women, 1900-1950* by Glenda Carlile.

Jane Jayroe

Miss America 1967

Third generation Oklahoman, Jane Jayroe became Oklahoma's second Miss America in 1966.

Jane was born in Clinton's Old Western Hospital to Pete and Helene Jayroe. At that time, her family lived in Hammon, Oklahoma, but soon moved to Sentinel and later to Laverne, which claims her as their native child. Her father was the boy's basketball coach and assistant principal, and her mother worked as an elementary school teacher.

Jane and her older sister Judy were involved in everything that went on in town. At the age of three, Jane begin singing in church, and took both piano and voice lessons. In high school she was a cheerleader, played in the band, and was a member of 4-H. She played on the basketball team that was first runner up for the state championship. She sang duets with classmate and friend Jimmy Webb, who later gained fame as a songwriter, writing such popular hits as *Up, Up, and Away* and *By the Time I get to Phoenix*.

Growing up she watched the Miss America Pageant on television in the family living room. Like most young girls she pretended to be Miss America, never dreaming she would one day hold that title.

In high school Jane changed the spelling of her first name to Jayne. When she entered college she had to use her legal name so reverted to the original spelling. When she traveled in the south she was often called Jayne Ann. Years later there is still confusion about the spelling of her name.

Jane chose to study at Oklahoma City University. She felt OCU not only provided first-rate training in music and fine arts, but also paid personal attention to its charges—not unlike the watchful eyes found in a small town.

At only sixteen, she entered and won her first beauty contest in Alva. As a freshman at Oklahoma City University, she was named queen of the All-college basketball tournament. In 1963, she entered the Miss Oklahoma City Contest for experience and before she knew it, she was Miss Oklahoma. At only nineteen she was on her way to being named Miss America. Jane has always felt she was too young to appreciate what was happening to her.

After a summer of practicing her talent, her mother and dad helped her pack the car and they left for Atlantic City. All three sat in the front seat as the back seat was loaded with bathing suits and evening gowns. A small town girl who had never been on an airplane, she believed she didn't stand a chance of winning against the sophistication and polish of the "big city girls." Later, she realized the all important pageant criteria of being oneself.

She competed in bathing suit and evening gown categories, then in talent and a question-and-answer session with master of ceremonies Bert Parks. Jane's talent included wearing tails, bow tie, and black sheer hose as she directed the Miss America Orchestra in the novelty tune "One, Two,

Jane Jayroe, Miss America. Photo, Courtesy of Jane Jayroe.

Three." Other state officials considered her performance a gimmick; thereafter, conducting the orchestra was eliminated as a talent selection.

Questions asked of Jane reflected the times: "What do you think of the Beatles?" and "What is your opinion on Vietnam?" The women's liberation movement had begun, and unbeknownst to her while she was walking the famous Miss America runway, outside convention hall, women burned bras in protest of the pageant.

When Burt Parks announced the winner, he said, "Oklahoma must be really jumping tonight." He was right. Celebrations were held in the dorms at OCU, in Laverne and across the state.

From the moment of her crowning, Miss America's official duties began. Jane was overwhelmed. She expected to return to her dorm room at OCU where she had already moved her belongings, but instead was caught in a whirlwind of press conferences, wardrobe fittings, and personal appearances. It was several weeks before she returned to her home state and celebrations in Tulsa, Oklahoma City, and Laverne. There was barely time for her to catch her breath, let alone visit with family and friends. During the next year, she made more than three hundred personal appearances in the United States, toured Vietnam, and visited seven European countries.

Decades later, Laverne is still proud as evidenced by Jane Jayroe Street. Jane laughed and quoted her nephew " in most towns the teen-agers drag Main Street. In Laverne they drag Jane."

The biggest thrill of her reign was being the first Miss America to visit and entertain U.S. troops in combat. She spent a week in Vietnam flying by helicopter to visit as many servicemen as possible. Pageant officials did not recommend the travel, but since then, Miss America's visit to the armed forces has been an annual event.

Jane earned an estimated $75,000 for public appearances that year in addition to a $10,000 scholarship.

Jane married Paul Peterson in 1968. When the couple divorced in 1976, she joined many other American women as a single working mother. The divorce was painful for Jane who was afraid she had let people down by not having a successful marriage.

Jane moved from Tulsa to Oklahoma City and worked for the educational television station, OETA. There, she produced a television show, beginning a 20 year career in journalism, administration, and public relations.

In 1978, she was asked to audition for the news co-anchor spot on KOCO-TV. When Jane was first hired by Channel 5, she was criticized as "just another pretty face" whose credibility as a newswoman was questionable. She soon proved her critics wrong and become one of Oklahoma's first and best known television news anchorwomen. The rise of "Five Alive News" in local ratings was remarkable.

Women were beginning to appear on news shows and Jane began on prime time. She said, "That would be unheard of today. I didn't have a journalism degree, didn't begin as a reporter, had little television programming experience, yet started out on the six and 10 o'clock news."

Viewers sometimes believe that the anchor simply walks into the newsroom and reads the script. Jane said, "Maybe some do. But for me, it was important to write my own news stories. I usually began shortly after noon preparing for the six o'clock broadcast".

"It is strange that the Miss America image opens doors, in terms of opportunities. But it's also a disadvantage to be stereotyped as a pretty face that doesn't have much behind it."

For a time she worked as anchorwoman on the NBC affiliate in Dallas. The pay was great and she received several prestigious journalism awards, including being the first female named "Outstanding News Personality" in the Dallas Television market. After four years, she moved back to Oklahoma City and the anchor spot on KOCO-TV 5. Although career opportunities were better in Dallas, she wanted her son to grow up in a smaller city close to her family and friends. Her desire was for him to have the community feeling she had loved so much.

In 1992, she became the first spokesperson for the Oklahoma Health Center and Vice President of the Presbyterian Health Foundation.

Four years later, she was the first woman to be elected chair of the Oklahoma Academy for State Goals, a statewide public policy think tank. That same year she became co-host of the weekly *Discover Oklahoma* television show promoting state tourism.

Governor Frank Keating, in 1999, appointed her cabinet secretary for Tourism and Recreation and Executive Director of the Oklahoma Tourism and Recreation Department. That also meant executive producer of the *Discover Oklahoma* show. As agency director she oversaw an annual budget of $58 million, which included the operation of 51 state parks, five state resorts, 11 golf courses and a variety of marketing and development programs. She held this position until she resigned in 2003 to become the spokesperson for Oklahoma City University's centennial celebration.

Jane enjoys writing and is the author of articles appearing in *McCall's* magazine, and *Chicken Soup for the Mother's Soul*. She has also published a book, *Out of the Blue, Delight Comes into Your Life*, and produced, "Daily Devotionals," a set of audio cassette tapes narrated by area ministers and laypeople. In 2006, a book written by Jane and Bob Burke, *More Grace than Glamour* was published to rave reviews.

An active volunteer, she has held leadership roles for several Civic and professional organizations. She serves on the Oklahoma City Community Foundation, Oklahoma City University Board of Trustees and the Oklahoma Centennial Commission. She was named one of *Oklahoma Today's* "100 Notable Women of Style."

Jane is a former trustee of the Sarkey's Foundation, and was appointed by Governor George Nigh to the commission on the Status of Women, by Governor Henry Bellmon to chair "Oklahoma Reunion '89'" and to the Legislative Compensation Board by Governor David Walters.

She is married to Gerald Gamble, a commercial real estate broker in Oklahoma City and a former chairman of the Greater Oklahoma City Chamber of Commerce.

Susan Powell

Miss America 1981

"Elk City Whoops" read the headlines of the *Daily Oklahoman* on September 7, 1980. The article continued, "relatives and friends of Susan Powell in this western Oklahoma town celebrated the crowning late Saturday of Elk City's favorite daughter as Miss America 1981, and said they anticipate a whopper of a party when Miss Powell returns from Atlantic City."

Susan Powell, Miss America. Photo, Courtesy of Vinita Powell, from the Author's collection.

All Oklahoma was proud when Susan Powell, a talented brunette, who sang an operatic aria into a telephone was crowned Miss America 1981. At 21, she was a senior in vocal performance at Oklahoma City University. The second Miss America from Oklahoma City University, Susan was the third from Oklahoma.

Like Jane Jayroe, Susan was a small town girl, raised almost as much by her community as her family. Born March 24, 1959, to Wendell and Vinita Powell, Susan joined a three-year old brother, Tom. The family lived on a farm near Elk City until Susan was three years old when they moved to town. Wendell, a successful landman in Oklahoma's booming oil and gas industry and Vinita, director of volunteers at the Elk City Hospital, were later divorced. Susan remained close to both her parents.

Elk City's favorite daughter grew up knee-deep in town life. By age two she was singing "Jesus Loves Me" before an audience. In high school she was cheerleader, drum major for the Pride of Western Oklahoma Band at Elk City High School, and a frequent actor in the Elk City Community Theater. Each week, for two years she traveled 160 miles round trip, to take classical vocal lessons in Oklahoma City.

Susan said, "My singing began in a children's choir at the United Methodist Church in Elk City when I was about 13 years old. I love audiences – I'm a big ham."

"It started as a dream and I followed that dream," she said. As a small child, she watched the televised pageant, then wrapped a sheet around her neck, and paraded through the house, singing, "There She Is, Miss America." People who knew her thought that might well be true some day.

In 1977, she was selected Miss Elk City and

second runner-up in the Miss Oklahoma Contest. After high school graduation she entered Oklahoma City University—primarily to continue with her vocal music teacher, Florence Birdwell. She received scholarships in both vocal music and trumpet at OCU. She sang with the Surrey Singers and played trumpet in the university band.

Nineteen-eighty was a banner year for Susan. She won the Metropolitan Opera Auditions and the Overall Artist award at the National Association of Teachers of Singing. In August, the twenty-four-year old college senior was named Miss Oklahoma and in September, Miss America.

Susan competed in the Miss Oklahoma contest three times before she won. She found that fulfilling that dream involved more than a pretty face, a perfect body, and a God-given talent. The commitment of time and energy to perfect those talents was enormous. By the time she was crowned Miss Oklahoma, Susan Powell had invested a total of twenty-five years in study of piano, trumpet, voice, theater, dance, and acting. Still, It hadn't seemed like work because she was doing what she loved.

Once Susan obtained the state title she was determined to win the national one. The time between the two competitions was short and hectic, with rehearsals, costume fittings, reading up on current events, and traveling to other states to observe their events.

Twenty-six singers competed in the talent competition for Miss America. As an accomplished operatic soprano, Susan took first place in Friday night's talent portion of the contest, with her rendition of "Lucy's Aria" from *The Telephone* by Menotti. Wearing a magenta bathing suit, the five-foot-four, 110 pound brunette also did well in the swim suit competition.

The 1980 pageant was memorable because of the dismissal of longtime emcee Bert Parks. Although not winners, for the first time two African-American women were finalists.

The outgoing queen Cheryl Prewitt crowned Susan the 54th Miss America before 20,000 people in Atlantic's City's Convention Hall. For the first time in many years Burt Parks did not sing the Miss America theme song. The pageant's new master of ceremonies was television's former Tarzan, Ron Ely.

Before the actual televised show, the contestants spend many hours of rehearsal even announcing a pretend Miss America. During the Saturday afternoon rehearsal, Ron Ely had pronounced Susan Powell as the new Miss America. That evening, when he opened the judges' envelope and discovered that Susan was the real winner, he was unnerved by the coincidence.

"Two time queen" Susan later joked to reporters, "I'm a little superstitious, but it was a wonderful rehearsal, wasn't it?" Since then more that one winner is announced at practice.

A celebrity panel of judges interviewed Susan. In addition to her music, the judges were interested in the fact that she was from western Oklahoma and that she had chopped cotton as a child. The interviews took place in private, and each girl was allowed a ten second statement on television, telling who she was and her ambition in life.

Back home in Elk City viewers watched in delight as "their girl" walked the famous runway. The Mayor said "Ninety percent of Elk City watched the pageant." When the winner was announced people cheered, some wept, and the honking of car horns was heard up and down Main Street. By morning, signs congratulating her appeared in store windows, and by Monday car bumper stickers proclaimed, *Elk City Loves You, Susan Powell.*

Grandmother Anna Powell joined 90 million other viewers when, with relatives and friends, she watched the telecast in her home. She told a newspaper reporter, "I was excited but not particularly surprised. I was expecting it."

She said her granddaughter began singing Jesus loves me when she was two. "She was always a happy child, sweet, kind, and loved to sing."

Elk City didn't have any idea of the changes in store for the small town. Postal employees delivered hundreds of letters to Susan's mother's house, many addressed to "Susan Powell, Miss America, Elk City, OK.

Tourists driving through town asked directions to her house. Many stopped and took pictures, and some were bold enough to walk to the porch and ring the bell.

After the coronation, Susan's life was a whirlwind for the next year. From the time of the crowning, she became the charge of the National Pageant officials. At the conclusion of her first newscast she presided at the Miss America Ball, falling into bed at 4:00 A.M. in the Miss America suite at Atlantic City's Regency Hotel. Two hours later she attended another news conference. Monday morning, in New York City, she appeared on *The Today Show* and *Good Morning, America.* She spent a month in the Miss America apartment in New York City being outfitted with a new wardrobe and making personal appearances.

In the first seven weeks of her reign, she traveled 30,000 miles and visited 16 states. "I love to travel," she said, "and I love meeting new people."

She confessed that one of the least desirable parts was living out of a suitcase and having to reset her watch. "But it's not bad," she said. "How can

I complain? I chose to be here and I love it."

Almost two months after her crowning she came home to Oklahoma. And what a homecoming that was! She flew into Tulsa to a large crowd of well-wishers including Governor Nigh, who proclaimed all of 1981 as Susan Powell Year in Oklahoma. In the rain, she rode in a downtown parade, and that night crowned Kathleen Allin the new Miss Oklahoma. The following day, in Oklahoma City, she attended a reception at OCU, made an appearance at the Kerr Center downtown, and at a Civic Center Music Hall luncheon where Mayor Patience Latting presented her with the keys to the city.

In Elk City, two billboards welcomed her. Normally, the town hosted a rodeo parade each year. That year they added a Miss America parade. Afterward, St. Matthew's Catholic Church volunteers served 6,000 cookies and gallons of punch. Town folks donated $6,500 to the celebration. Susan found time to sing at a wedding for friends before heading on to St. Louis, Chicago, and Seattle.

Susan's year as Miss America was relatively calm. Ronald Reagan was elected President and the nation took a conservative swing. She observed, "The Miss America Pageant is the height of establishment, it fit in very well with that era." For her year's work, she earned $100,000 cash and $30,000 in scholarships.

Susan began her professional career the day after relinquishing her crown, when she joined the Seattle Opera Company. She debuted as Adele in *Die Fledermaus*. Since then, she has sung with the New York City Opera, the Boston Pops, and has starred in theaters, opera houses and concert halls. Her versatility makes her sought after for operetta and musical comedy. Susan has been seen in such roles as Laurie in *Oklahoma*, Eliza Doolittle in *My*

Fair Lady, Julie Jordan in *Carousel,* Magnolia in *Show-boat,* Sarah in *Guys and Dolls,* and Nellie Forbush in *South Pacific.*

As fate would have it, she met her husband, opera singer David Parsons, at the Cincinnati Opera, where they played the leading roles in *Oklahoma!* They were married in 1986 in Elk City, Oklahoma, and live in Manhattan.

From, 1993 until 2006, Susan hosted her own half-hour television series, "Home Matters" on the Discovery channel, a top rated cable network show that featured home decorating, cooking, gardening segments, and a variety of crafts projects. She has captivated audiences across the country with her charm and enthusiasm.

She appears across the country in concerts and musical theater. In September 2001 she sang with the New Japan Philharmonic at a pops concert in Tokyo. That same year she was the guest soloist with the Utah Symphony in Salt Lake City.

In addition, Susan serves as a corporate spokesperson, for Gillette's Personal Care Division, "Made in America Clothing", Phillips Petroleum, and Ford Motor Company.

In 1981, Susan was presented the Pioneer Woman Award at the 5th annual Pioneer Woman ceremony at the Marland Renaissance Ball in Ponca City. At the 2002 annual Oklahoma Hall of Fame Awards, she was named Ambassador of Good Will for the State of Oklahoma.

Active with an organization of former Miss Americas who perform for benefit shows, she has returned to the pageant as a judge and co-host. In 1995, both Susan and Jane Jayroe attended the seventy-fifth anniversary of the Miss America pageant and watched the crowning of fellow Oklahoman, Shawntel Smith.

She co-hosted the 2005 Miss America preliminary competition. Susan joined the three other Miss Americas from Oklahoma in Tulsa for the homecoming celebration for Jennifer Berry, Oklahoma's fifth Miss America.

Her advice to the new Miss America was, "Write, write, write. Write down what you do every day because you think you're going to remember everything, and there's no way you can do it. I would keep a journal. Those would be my three words of advice."

Susan has found her Oklahoma upbringing to be a good foundation for life in New York City. Strong roots have given her the strength to survive in this "make it or break it town." She enjoys frequent trips back to Oklahoma, often appearing with the Philharmonic or just visiting with family and friends.

Shawntel Smith

Miss Oklahoma 1996

When Lacricia Shawntel Smith woke on Sunday, September 17, 1995, she looked around the magnificent Miss America suite in Atlantic City and saw the Miss America crown on the dresser. Not only a year older since the day before, she was now Miss America, 1996. On her 24th birthday, she had become the fourth Oklahoman to wear the crown.

Back home, the small town of Muldrow buzzed. Just recently a sign was installed at the outskirts of town declaring, "Welcome to Muldrow, the home of *Miss Oklahoma*, Shawntel Smith". Now the sign would need to be changed to " the home of *Miss America".*

The night before, every television set in the Sequoyah County town of 2,500 people was tuned to the Miss America contest. The Mayor's home telephone started ringing immediately after Shawntel received the title and didn't stop all the next day. Anyone in Muldrow will tell you, "The crowning of hometown girl Shawntel Smith is just about the most exciting thing that has ever happened in this county."

Townspeople are quick to say they weren't surprised. They had always expected great things to happen to their hard-working, favorite daughter. Pretty, friendly and thoughtful, Shawntel Smith was described as "the kind of girl you would want your daughter to be." In elementary and middle school, she took piano lessons and played softball. One softball team went all the way to the state tournament. She won the President's physical fitness medal and was a cheerleader in high school and in college.

Shawntel said, "I was a tomboy. I wasn't the prettiest girl in school."

The daughter of Galen and Karen Smith, Shawntel has a younger brother, Michael, and sister, Carisa. Like her siblings, Shawntel worked in the family business, Smith's Furniture Store on U.S. 64 in Roland. The Smith family was close, and involved in their church. The parents instilled in each child a sense of uniqueness, and the assurance that they could obtain any goal they set for themselves.

Shawntel's ambition was to be the first woman in her family to graduate from college. Convinced that pageant scholarships could finance her dream, the high school senior entered and won her first title as Muldrow's Senior Miss. Her friends talked her into competing with the rest of the girls in the senior class. When she won, she thought that would be the last of her beauty contests.

In nearby Ft. Smith, Arkansas, Shawntel attended Westark Community College. The activities director there asked her to enter the college pageant. Intending to focus on her studies, she declined. Again, a friend persuaded Shawntel to compete with her. The selling point was that even if they didn't win they would receive $250 for entering. That would buy a lot of books. She placed second runner-up and received a one-year tuition scholarship. The next year she competed again and won fourth runner-up and another year of tuition.

After graduating from the two year Westark program she transferred to Northeastern State University in Tahlequah, where she won the Miss NSU pageant. This enabled her to compete for the Miss Oklahoma title. In the next two years, she placed in the top ten in both the Miss Muskogee and the Miss Stroud pageants. Still, she felt that beauty contest were not for her. Shawntel concentrated on her schoolwork.

At NSU, she completed her Bachelors degree in business and marketing and was hired as the marketing director at Northeastern State University Muskogee Campus. She received a phone call from the Miss Oklahoma pageant committee telling her they had neglected to inform her she had received a scholarship to Oklahoma City University. Able to apply that money toward tuition for her master's degree, she enrolled at OCU. She again received a phone call from a state pageant official, this time encouraging her to enter the Miss Tulsa State Fair contest. This would be the last contest she would be eligible for before aging out. Shawntel entered, won the Miss Tulsa State Fair, then the Miss Oklahoma contest, and in September, 1995 she was crowned Miss America 1996.

Shawntel has said in interviews, "If your dreams and goals don't happen overnight just keep working on them." Her main goal was obtaining

Shawntel Smith, Miss America. Photo by Andrew Eccles. Courtesy of Karen Smith (from the Author's collection).

scholarship money and through the many contests, she received over $75,000 in academic assistance.

Five foot three and one-half- inch tall, the blue-eyed beauty was the first redhead to win the Miss America title in fifty-one years. The third Oklahoma City University student to win the title, she was the fourth recipient from Oklahoma. In 1995, OCU also claimed title holders for Mrs America and Miss Black America. Shawntel was thrilled that Oklahoma's two former Miss Americas, Jane Jayroe and Susan Powell were both in attendance at her coronation in Atlantic City.

For the talent portion of her competition, Shawntel sang the show tune "Woman in the Moon" from the Barbra Streisand remake of the movie, *A Star is Born.*

By the mid-1990's, emphasis in the Miss America contest shifted from talent to the interview with questions based on personal goals and social issues. In 1995, a new category called personal platform was added. Each state contender chose an issue of importance and supported that issue during in-depth interviewing. The candidate was evaluated on her commitment. Shawntel chose and promoted her platform "School to Work: The Key to Keeping Kids in School".

As Miss America, Shawntel promoted her School to Work Program across the country. The U.S. Department of Education and Labor appointed her as the National School to Work Ambassador to America's youth. She was able to forge partnerships between states, regions, labor, students, teachers, parents and community leaders to create ways of learning that were not only school-based but also work-based. The participation of states grew from seven at the beginning of her reign to all 50 states at the end of her year.

Soon after Shawntel was crowned, newspaper reporters recognized her cool headedness and high level of energy. Ten minutes after the telecasts' end she addressed the press, then spoke to the state Miss America volunteers, then the national sponsors. "You would have thought she had been doing this her whole life," said Marilyn Feehan, chairman of the Atlantic City Hostess Committee.

In one particular day she addressed two New Jersey High Schools, the New Jersey State Senate and Assembly separately, signed autographs, lunched with a handful of assemblymen and senators and that night spoke to 500 Miss America volunteers. Often her schedule was so full, she lunched in the limo on her favorite peanut butter and jelly sandwich.

One day, she spoke at a breakfast in Anaheim, California, and at a dinner in Washington, DC. Not bad for a girl, who before she was named Miss America, had rarely given a speech and had never seen the Atlantic Ocean.

All America was interested in this beautiful young girl from Oklahoma.

Earlier that year, on May 19th, the Alfred P. Murrah building in Oklahoma City had been bombed. Shawntel found that people needed to know how Oklahoma was faring and wanted to express their sympathies. On her state's behalf, she thanked people across the world for their efforts and condolences.

Having been described as bubbly, Shawntel claimed that was overkill. "I just always see the bright side of things and respond positively to life." However, her smile has been described as "lighting up a room."

Making speeches and other public appearances, Shawntel traveled an estimated 20,000 miles and earned some $250,000 in fees. She received a $40,000 scholarship from the Miss America Pageant along with a $12,000 scholarship from the Miss Oklahoma pageant. To opponents of beauty pageants she points out that the scholarship money is a wonderful way for young girls to pay for their college education.

For a time, after her year as Miss America, she co-hosted with Jim Buratti, *Discover Oklahoma*, the weekly statewide television show promoting Oklahoma Tourism.

Shawntel has had the dents in her rhinestone-studded tiara repaired three times not because she is clumsy, but because the school kids like to try it on and frequently drop it. She said it's worth it to see the children's eyes light up when she says, "You can do it."

Still one of the most sought after motivational speakers, she travels around the country sharing her message of faith, focus, and follow through. She speaks on a variety of topics including leadership, good ethics, and setting goals.

She and her husband Ryan Wuerch live in Raleigh, North Carolina, with their three sons.

Shawntel returned to Oklahoma for the unveiling of the statue of Oklahoma City University's three Miss Americas during OCU's "Centennial Celebration of the Century". She was back again for the homecoming celebration in Tulsa when Jennifer Berry was honored as Oklahoma's fifth Miss America.

In 1997, Shawntel's mother and manager, who was also her best friend, was killed in a tragic automobile accident. She survived that difficult time with the help of fellow Miss Americas. She said, "Such bonds are a lasting perk of the title. I wasn't in a sorority in college, but I am now."

Jennifer Berry

Miss America 2006

Jennifer Berry was destined to become Miss America. When she was born, her grandfather, the late William Hamilton, presented her with a T-shirt that read "Miss America 2003". He missed his prediction by only three years.

On January 21, 2006, this University of Oklahoma co-ed became the fifth Oklahoman to wear the Miss America crown. The twenty-two year old beauty from Tulsa is an aspiring elementary school teacher.

Jennifer's win destroyed the myth that Oklahoma's Miss Americas are always small town girls. Previous state winners won the competition as singers - Jennifer is a dancer. Three of the others have studied at OCU – Jennifer attends the University of Oklahoma.

Another difference in 2006 was that the 85-year-old Miss America pageant traded the boardwalk for the Las Vegas strip. In a bid to revive interest it was moved from Atlantic City to the Aladdin Hotel in Las Vegas. The pageant also was postponed from September, 2005, to January, 2006, because of these changes.

The delay worked to Jennifer's advantage giving her the opportunity to hone her speaking skills at 85 school assemblies.

The closer city enabled 130 friends, relatives, and Oklahoma pageant representatives to attend and show Jennifer their support.

Miss America 1967, Jane Jayroe, watched the pageant on television and was excited but not surprised to see Jennifer crowned. She said. "I attended the Miss Oklahoma pageant last June in Tulsa, and I was extremely impressed with her as a contestant."

Kay Alexander, executive director of the Miss Oklahoma Pageant said, "It was a good week. Jennifer did well in all the preliminaries."

Jennifer won the talent competition performing a ballet *en point* to the music "Within". She was first runner up for the Quality of Life award, which is based on the contestant's platforms.

Her platform issue was: Building intolerance to drunk driving and underage drinking. As a teenager, she had adopted that cause, when she lost a friend in an alcohol-related accident.

The night of the pageant Jennifer appeared relaxed. She pirouetted beautifully and answered her questions well and with a little humor. Oklahoman's watching on TNN began calling friends – "I think Oklahoma is going to win."

Selected over 51 other women, she earned a $30,000 college scholarship and a year- long speaking tour.

"This is an honor, this is surreal," Jennifer said. "I don't believe it right now. Hopefully it will sink in, maybe tomorrow. It's a dream come true, but more importantly it's a job that I'm honored to have."

She seemed a natural, but friends in Jenks and the University of Oklahoma know it has been five years of competing and hard work.

Jennifer had begun studying ballet at the age of three. When she was nine she studied at prestigious companies like the Pacific Northwest Ballet in Seattle, the Peoria Ballet in Illinois, and the Tulsa Ballet. At eleven, she received full summer scholarships to study with the David Howard Dance Center of New York.

When Jennifer was thirteen she created a

successful summer dance workshop in Tulsa with two of her friends. Three summers later, they taught over one hundred students. Throughout high school, Jennifer taught ballet to students from ages four to fourteen.

At the age of fifteen, her life changed forever. The wreck that killed her friend was alcohol related. The most difficult part was knowing her friend's death could have been prevented. Sorrow motivated her to try to save others from losing their lives through a senseless decision. She became an avid volunteer and spokesperson for MADD (Mothers Against Drunk Driving). Through the Victims Impact Panel, Jennifer spoke to DUI offenders as part of their rehabilitation.

In 2001, Jennifer graduated from Jenks High School where she was a member of the National Honor Society and active in Student Council and Key Club, a community service organization. She was also a member of the varsity pom squad. As a senior she served as president of the Family Career and Community Leaders of America.

At the University of Oklahoma Jennifer was a member of Projects Under 21 and served on the first student committee board for the university's *Think - If You Drink* program. She spoke to hundreds of incoming college freshman regarding the dangers of alcohol and to hundreds of elementary students about good decision making and creating healthy life styles.

She made the Dean's Honor roll in 2002 and 2003, and the President's honor roll in 2004 and 2005.

Attending OU provided an opportunity for Jennifer to study with the acclaimed University of Oklahoma School of Dance. In 2005, she guest performed with the Tulsa Opera along with five other school of dance performers.

Jennifer's love of dancing and interest in the Miss America Organization, led her to the Miss Oklahoma Pageant. In 2001, at only seventeen years of

Jennifer Berry, Miss America 2006. Photo Courtesy of Miss Oklahoma Association.

age, she received a non-finalist talent award. The next year, she was a top ten semi-finalist and a preliminary swimsuit winner. In 2003, Jennifer placed third runner-up and received a preliminary swimsuit award. In 2004, she received third place in the Kiwanis Club Community Service Award, again placing third runner up. After competing for five years, Jennifer competed as Miss Grand Lake and then captured the title of Miss Oklahoma. She won the preliminary awards in swimsuit, talent, and interview, along with the first place Kiwanis Club Community Service Award.

Since her crowning as Miss America, she has traveled to New York, Atlantic City, Kansas City, Philadelphia, and Washington. She visited children's hospitals, car shows, and was interviewed on all the major television talk shows. She appeared at the NCAA basketball finals and threw out the first ball at the Baltimore Orioles baseball game.

A month passed before Jennifer returned to Oklahoma. She was welcomed back to Tulsa, February 23, for a homecoming celebration. Honoring her at a luncheon was Tulsa Mayor Bill LaFortune who declared Friday, February 23, as Miss America Day in Tulsa.

That evening, she joined former Miss Americas from Oklahoma, Jane Jayroe, Susan Powell, and Shawntel Smith at the Miss America Gala held at the Oklahoma Aquarium in Jenks.

The final event of her Tulsa homecoming was the Miss America Revue at the Jenks Public School Performing Arts Center. The four Miss Americas shared experiences in an onstage chat, and other Miss America top ten finalists performed their talents. To a standing ovation Jennifer crowned her successor, the new Miss Oklahoma, Jennifer Warren. Over seven hundred people attended.

On Monday, capping off the full weekend, Jennifer was honored by the Oklahoma Senate and House of Representatives. She gave her support to a proposed law, tightening penalties on those who sell beer to minors. She said the legislation would help reduce underage drinking but that Oklahomans must reduce the misconception that drinking alcohol was a youth's rite of passage.

Some people assume that when she completes her tour as Miss America, Jennifer will move out of state, but she says that's not in her plans. She relayed to a newspaper correspondent, "I love Oklahoma, and I miss Oklahoma."

Clara Luper, Civil Rights Leader. Photo, Courtesy of Research Division of the Oklahoma Historical Society.

Clara Luper

Mother of the Civil Rights Movement

On August 19, 1958, Clara Luper led a dozen black children into Katz Drug Store in downtown Oklahoma City, and ordered thirteen soft drinks to be consumed at the counter. The children were refused service. The first of a series of lunch counter sit-ins, the peaceful demonstrations that followed would last five years and eleven months. This was the first major civil rights demonstration of the 1960's and the longest nonviolent, concentrated movement in America's history.

In her book, *Behold the Walls*, Clara Luper recalled that hot August night in 1958, "I thought about my father who had died in 1957 in the Veterans Hospital and who had never been able to sit down and eat a meal in a decent restaurant. I remembered how he used to tell us that someday he would take us to dinner and to parks and zoos. And when I asked him when was someday, "Someday will be real soon", he would always say as tears ran down his cheeks.

So my answer was, 'Yes, tonight is the night. History compels us to go, and not let history alone be our final judge."

Clara was speaking to the group of NAACP Youth Council members who had congregated at her home in Oklahoma City. For eighteen months the group had been studying non-violence as a way of overcoming injustices. Now they were ready to take a stand.

These same youth had been on a trip north and were surprised to find that in New York City and other towns along the way blacks could eat in the same cafes and sleep in the same hotels as the white people. During Negro History Week, as it was called then, Clara had written, and the students performed the play *Brother President*, the story of Martin Luther King, Jr. and the non-violent techniques used to eliminate segregation in Montgomery, Alabama. First presented at Dunjee High School, the all black school where Clara taught, the play was so well received it was performed in various venues across the state.

Herbert Wright, the NAACP National Youth Director, saw the play in 1957, at the East 6th St. Christian Church. Impressed, he invited the cast to present it in New York City at a "Salute to Young Freedom Fighters Rally."

Clara directed the bus driver to take the northern route to New York City and to return by way of the southern route. The cast of 26 students, most of which had never been outside of Oklahoma City, stopped in St. Louis for dinner and experienced their first integrated lunch counter. The group stayed at the Henry Hudson Hotel in New York City and were entertained in both Manhattan and Harlem before traveling to Washington, D.C. In the nation's capitol they took in the usual tourist sites, including Arlington Cemetery. Watching the changing of the guard, the group pledged that they would do something for their country.

As the greyhound bus traveled west, the walls of segregation again appeared. In Nashville, they could not find a place to sit down and eat. Paper sack lunches became the order of the day through Tennessee, Arkansas, and Oklahoma.

The students began talking about the "Sooner" State. *The sooner we get rid of segregation the better off we will be.*

Back in Oklahoma City, they decided their project would be to eliminate segregation in public accommodations, no matter how long it took. The campaign began with small groups of two or three people attempting to eat at local establishments. Approaches were made to the City Manager and the City Council, and they launched a letter writing campaign to churches. None of these efforts were successful.

The children were taught to be respectful no matter what - even if they were spit on and cursed or struck. The young people were clean, neatly dressed, always with hair brushed and shoes shined.

Now, the twelve children, ranging from six years old to fifteen, were ready to try to drink a Coca Cola in a public store. Blacks were allowed to shop at Katz Drug Store and could order sandwiches and drinks but they were placed in a paper sacks and must be eaten in the streets.

On this occasion, the young people sat on the stools in "for whites only" territory. One of the older girls, Barbara Posey, spoke. "We'd like thirteen Cokes, please."

"You may have them to go," the waitress said nervously.

Barbara placed a five dollar bill on the counter. "We'll drink them here."

Soon, police surrounded the group. White customers left, their food untouched, and a hostile crowd gathered yelling racial slurs. The teacher and her students held their ground. After a while, her group peacefully left. The next day more young people showed up at Clara's home, ready to go back. In two days Katz announced that its 38 outlets in Missouri, Oklahoma, Kansas, and Iowa would serve all people regardless of race, creed, or color. The children loved ordering and eating hamburgers and French fries at the lunch counter.

In *Behold the Walls,* Clara said, "Blacks were not allowed to sit down at any lunch counter to eat. Blacks were to sweep around the seats, and keep them clean so whites could sit down. It didn't make any difference what kind of white person it was, thief, rapist, murderer, uneducated, the only requirement was that he or she be white...Nor did it make any difference what kind of black you were, B.A. Black; M.A. Black; Ph.D. Black; rich Black; poor Black; young Black; old Black; pretty Black, you were not to sit down."

The next day, at Veazey's Drug Store they were met at the door by the manager who welcomed them and told them the new policy was that the eating facilities were open to all people. Barriers were beginning to come down, but it would take a long time for the next ones to fall.

Clara Luper had spent her whole life behind walls of prejudice and mis-understandings. She was born May 3, 1923, in Okfuskee County and educated in the segregated schools of Hoffman and Grayson in Okmulgee County. She remembers using textbooks with missing pages that had been discarded from the white schools, sitting at the back of trains, and being excluded from restaurants, libraries, bathrooms and even phone booths. Blacks were not allowed to try on clothes in stores. Clara remembers her mother buying her a pair of shoes that didn't fit because she could not try them on. A sign in nearby Henryetta, said "Negroes, read and run, if you can't read, run anyway."

Her parents, Ezell and Isabell Shepard were uneducated. Her father fought in World War I and was a hard worker who always saw a better day coming. Her mother was much more cautious. While living in Texas, she had seen a black man burned and she was afraid of white people.

Isabell worked as a maid for Mrs. Lackey in Hoffman, Oklahoma.. She also ironed white folk's clothes. Clara remembers taking the clothing to the back door because she was not permitted at the front of the house. She recalls sitting in the back of the train and asking why. Her mother looked to see if anyone had heard and told her to shut up, but her dad replied, "Someday you'll ride in the front." In Henrietta, blacks were not allowed in town after dark.

Clara's parents taught her that she was as good as anybody, and although she might dislike her circumstances, not to hate the people. The family was so busy trying to survive they didn't have time to build resentments.

Her brother, Ulysses, was about ten years old when he contacted pneumonia. Ezell took him to Henrietta, but blacks couldn't be admitted to the all white hospital. He carried him to the white doctor's office but Ulysses died after the white doctors refused to see him.

Hazel and Oneita were Clara's sisters. Clara and Oneita graduated in the top five of their senior class at Grayson High School. There were only five students in the class.

While attending college in Langston, Clara discovered another kind of prejudice. Although in an all black school, Clara felt discriminated against because they were too poor to live on campus or pledge a sorority. Her friend, Ada Lois Sipuel later became nationally known as the first black to attend the University of Oklahoma Law School. At Langston they'd had some good debates.

With a bachelor's degree from Langston University, Clara and one other were the first black students to enroll in the social studies department at the University of Oklahoma. There, she received an MA. One professor told her he "had never taught a nigger and never wanted to."

After graduation, Clara taught social studies in schools in Taft, Pawnee, and at segregated Dunjee High School in Oklahoma City. At Dungee, she became the advisor for the youth group of the NAACP and spent the next seven years working to integrate eating establishments.

She wondered at so many expressions of hatred. After all, Oklahoma is the buckle on the Bible Belt.

John A. Brown's Department Store became the Bunker Hill of the sit-in movement. Protests began on August 27, 1958, and lasted until 1961. For three years, Clara tried to talk to Mrs. John A. Brown and the storeowner refused to let her. In 1961, when Mrs. Brown asked her to come to her office, Clara was tempted to refuse the invitation. The two powerful women, from such different ways of life, ended up in tears and in each other's arms.

In 1958, Clara was jailed 26 times. She said, "Being arrested is a humiliating experience that makes you feel like you committed the worst crime. You lose things that are precious to you, like your pocketbook and your pride.

But then you are able to connect with people who have gone to jail for freedom. If you can look at the cell and smell the aroma of a jail and look to a better day...I could see above the jail cell."

As a teacher, this experience made her better qualified to tell kids to stay out of prison. Clara said, "If you believe in a cause, you cannot destroy beliefs."

In the next few years, the Anna Maude Cafeterias, Bishops, the Split T restaurants and others were tough walls to crack, but all ended up integrated.

Mayor Norick of Oklahoma City was no help, nor was the city council, or the political establishments who believed that owners of private business's had the right to refuse service to whoever they wished. When the sit-ins started, there was tremendous opposition even from some African Americans. By 1961, whites had joined the demonstrations, and Oklahomans came to realize civil rights were more important than property rights. In 1962 and 1963 sit-ins continued daily in the summer time, after school and on weekends. June 2, 1964, the Oklahoma City Council passed the public accommodation ordinance.

On July 3, 1964, blacks tested four eating establishments and were served at all of them. The sit-in campaign ended five years and 11 months after it started.

Clara's next target was the white churches many of which did not allow blacks to attend worship services. The sit-in tactic worked. Fair housing was another target of discrimination. Oklahoma City passed its fair housing ordinance in 1969.

During the next few years, Clara went to Tulsa and Lawton and helped with their discrimination problems, marched at Selma, Alabama, and ran for the Democratic nomination for the United States Senate. She came in sixth in a field of eleven.

Clara recalls that the news coverage changed over the years. At first the editors and reporters were afraid of the NAACP. *The Daily Oklahoman* was anti-black, but when the owners saw the demonstrations were truly non-violent the press began writing articles endorsing the movement. On E.K. Gaylord's 100th birthday he called Clara and asked her to come to his office. He stood up from his desk and shook her hand.

Clara went back to teaching school. During the early integration efforts of Oklahoma City Schools, she was transferred from the all black Dungee High School to the all white Northwest Classen. The days that followed were filled with hate calls and threats. She was constantly told that "no nigger jailbird" would teach at Northwest Classen High School.

Her first day was memorable. As she walked to her classroom, a group of white 9th graders stood at the end of the hallway. They began to chant: "Here comes a nigger. Here comes a nigger." She approached them and said, "My name is Mrs. Clara Luper, and remember I'm your teacher."

The young men lowered their heads and apologized. She never had another problem with the students.

However, demonstrations were staged outside her classroom against bussing, and groups paraded up and down outside her windows. "Nigger, get out of our classroom".

The white students put their arms around her and said, "This is our teacher and if she leaves this classroom, we'll leave too".

Clara taught at Northwest Classen for two years, then she was transferred to Northeast High, and finally John Marshall High School. It is no surprise that former students describe her as tough.

Clara has received over one hundred awards, citations and academic honors. She says the awards do not go to her but to the hundreds of people who believed in the cause.

She was the first Black Vice-President of both the Oklahoma County Teachers Association and the Oklahoma City Social Science Teacher's Association. She was inducted into the Oklahoma Afro-American Hall of Fame in 1986, and the Oklahoma Women's Hall of Fame in 1993. On July 16, 2000, The Clara Luper Corridor, a street in Oklahoma City was named for her.

Clara is still in contact with the original sit-inners and says she is so proud that they've all gone to college and have successful careers: Richard Brown is a retired teacher in Oklahoma City; Elmer Edwards is a social worker in Sacramento; Linda Pogue is in public relations in Washington, D.C.; Lana Pogue owns a business in Baltimore; Areda Tolliver is a teacher in Cincinnati; Calvin Luper is a photographer; Marilyn Luper owns an All State Insurance Company; and Portwood Williams Jr. is retired from the post office,

The new Oklahoma History Center has an exhibit featuring an exact likeness of the Katz Drug Store lunch counter. Visitors from all over the world can now see what a difference was made by one woman and a dozen children.

June Brooks, The Wild Ma'am of Ardmore. Photo,
Courtesy of June Brooks.

June Brooks

The Mad Ma'am from Ardmore

Hired in 1942 as the first female landman, June Brooks later founded her own Oil and Gas Company. As the self proclaimed defender of the oil industry, calling herself the "The Mad Ma'am from Ardmore', she traveled three million air miles, visited fifty states, lobbied Capitol Hill, and made hundreds of speeches urging the deregulation of oil and adoption of a national energy policy.

June Brooks was born and raised in Ardmore, in the Southern oil patch area of Oklahoma. Her parents were in the grocery business. Her first job was secretary at the first Baptist Church where she received $10 a week in pay.

When offered the job as Magnolia Oil's landman she was thrilled. She went to work for $165 per month plus cost of living advances. Most girls in the area worked at the nearby air base and were making $50 a month.

Oil companies didn't usually hire women in those days, but in1942, most available men were in the service.

A man at Magnolia, later Mobile Oil, was doing land work from an Ardmore office. He took June under his wing and trained her to do his job before he died.

Three years later, her Navy Ace fiancé was killed in the war. June quit her job with Magnolia to go back to school. She attended North Texas State Teachers College in Denton, Texas. She majored in music with the dream of someday becoming the world's greatest opera singer. Instead she met and married Ben Brooks, who worked in the first well drilled in the Gulf of Mexico by Kerr McGee and Magnolia. Eventually, they opened their own independent oil company. She worked alongside her husband as a landman, wildcatter, and a partner in every aspect of the business for 27 years. The marriage ended in divorce, and at the age of 50, June began a new career. She was secretary-treasurer of Beaver Oil and Gas Company prior to founding her own firm, the June Brooks Oil and Gas Company.

She threw herself into the male world of independent oilmen, and in 1974 became the fourth woman to join the 600-men Oklahoma Landman Association.

In 1975, she was the only registered woman delegate to the World Petroleum Congress in Tokyo. That conference motivated her to go on the road preaching energy independence for the United States. "In Asia, I had a chance to see how the rest of the world is living. It made me appreciate the United States. I hadn't paid my dues to the free enterprise system. I decided to do my little bit to help save it."

Her "little bit" became a one-woman nationwide campaign for a working practical national energy policy to provide the United States with an uninterrupted domestic energy supply. She wanted to remove the country from dependence on foreign crude.

She said, "People asked me why didn't I get out and start making speeches, so I did.

A vice-president of Chevron in San Francisco helped write her first speech, and a Broadway director and author helped translate it into terms people who weren't in the oil business would understand.

For the next thirty years, calling herself the "Mad Ma'am from Ardmore", she traveled to 50 states, logging three million air miles, making public speeches, and giving radio, television and press interviews that were widely publicized in the local and national media, urging the deregulation of oil. She spoke at schools, universities, service clubs, civic organizations, state legislatures, and lobbied the halls of Capitol Hill.

Initially this traveling was at her own expense, but when the campaign became so large, she accepted payment for her speaking engagements and contributions from individuals and energy groups.

Her approach was simple and direct: go to the people and tell it like it is, give them a decorated paper sack full of literature, a "Mad" campaign button, two postcards and a pencil. That way, each person could dash off notes to his U.S. Senator and Congressman on the spot.

June emphasized that she was not speaking only for the oil industry but for the preservation of free enterprise.

John Taylor, an affiliate with the Energy Advocates organization, said he has never known anyone who could carry a story to the public as well. He said, "We have a lot of outstanding people in the industry, I'm not alone in voicing this, June Brooks really was a great testifier in representing the oil industry.

Her success in meeting with top officials is evidenced in the photographs she has of herself with various celebrities including Presidents Reagan and Bush, Governor's Bellmon and Nigh, news personalities Tom Brokaw, Douglas Edwards, Sam Donaldson, Mike Wallace, Andrea Mitchell, Ted Turner, and Jack Anderson. She also has pictures of herself with Elizabeth Dole and Norman Vincent Peale.

Oil has been June's life. "In the oil industry I've been on top financially and scraping the bottom several times but that's what I love about the industry. I hate that Las Vegas kind of gambling, but many a time I've taken everything I had and bet it on the chance of pumping some oil out of the ground."

At times, being a woman in a man's world was difficult but at other times it opened doors that would otherwise have been closed. She was elected to the board of directors of the Independent Petroleum Association of America and received the 1978 Special Service Award for Distinguished Service from the American Association of Petroleum Landmen.

An expert in her field, June received the Outstanding Women in Energy Award from the Women in Energy, the Distinguished Service Award from the Oklahoma Petroleum Council, and the Oklahoma Petroleum Council Speakers Bureau Award 1978 through 1982.

In 1982, June was one of the first eight women inducted into the Oklahoma Women's Hall of Fame by the Oklahoma Commission on the Status of Women. That same year she received the Woman in the News Award from the Oklahoma Hospitality Club.

She received the Pioneer Woman Award, in 1984, at the Marland Renaissance Ball in Ponca City. In presenting the award, Governor George Nigh said, "June Brooks, is one of the neat women in Oklahoma, particularly in the field of energy. She is an appropriate recipient of the Pioneer Woman Award because she is truly a pioneer in this area.

She has received a lot of national attention for her efforts in energy. She is the head of her own company, and she is... the spirit! Not only is she the spirit in energy, but she is the spirit of enthusiasm for Oklahoma."

Dr. John Robinson, chairman of the E.W. Marland Estate Commission said, " The Commission is pleased to recognize June Brooks as the 1984 Pioneer Woman recipient. She represents the spirit of all our pioneer women, who continue to contribute so much to our state and nation."

June has three children; Claudia Brooks Kittrell, Ardmore; Rebecca Brawley, Oklahoma City, and William Ben Brooks, who lives in New York City.

The influence of June in the oil industry is still felt. In 2005, she was presented the Lifetime Achievement Award from the International Energy Advocates during the 13th annual energy policy conference in Denver, Colorado. Her daughters flew her to Denver to accept the award. She appreciated the award and seeing so many old friends.

June admits to being 82 years old. She looks like she is 60 and still has that energy that has made her an Oklahoma legend.

Wanda Jackson, Queen of Rockabilly. Photo, Courtesy of Wanda Jackson.

Wanda Jackson

"Queen of Rockabilly"

Wanda Jackson's career began when she was a high school student in Oklahoma City. The legendary Hank Thompson heard her perform on the radio and helped her land a 1954 recording contract. Elvis Presley encouraged her to add rock elements to her country music, and she became known as the "Queen of Rockabilly." Fifty years later, she is still a sought after performer.

In 2005, Oklahoma City's Wanda Jackson received the nation's highest honor in folk and traditional arts from the National Endowment for the Arts

Not bad for a girl from Maude, Oklahoma. Born on October 20, 1937, Wanda was the daughter of Tom and Nellie Jackson.

Her mother has been credited with starting her on her music career. As a toddler, she put her in the bathtub and told her to sing loud so she could hear her and know she was all right. Wanda started singing and hasn't quit yet.

The work situation in Oklahoma forced the family to move, for a while to California, where her father worked for North American Aviation. He also went to barber school, and her mother worked as an interior decorator.

Her parents loved country music and attended western swing band dances at local ballrooms. Parents often took their children with them. Wanda stood by the stage in awe of the musicians and the female singers. She announced that she wanted to be a "girl" singer.

Her father was pleased with her interest in music and bought her a Stella guitar. Just six years old, he began teaching her chords and encouraged her love of music. A self-taught musician, he played the fiddle and the guitar. He had met her mother when he played for a band at the Union Hall in Maude on Saturday nights.

Her mother was homesick and concerned for an invalid mother so they moved back to Oklahoma. Her father consented to the move but said, "You'll have to help me make a living and if you ever make the gravy out of water, we're moving back to California."

The family made their home in South Oklahoma City where her father drove a taxi and her mother worked as a seamstress for an interior decorating company. Wanda attended Crooked Oak Elementary School and Capitol Hill Junior and Senior High Schools. She sang for school assemblies and on other occasions.

A cousin taught her to yodel while riding horseback. Wanda reported later that this is the best way to learn yodeling, out on the south forty, bouncing on a horse.

In the ninth grade, she wrote her first song, *If You Knew What I Know,* followed by *You'd Be The First To Know.*

In 1951, the local radio station KLPR in Capitol Hill sponsored a talent show. Wanda won and was given her own fifteen-minute show while still in high school. She said the kids laughed at her when she walked down the hall carrying her guitar. The boy's asked her if she was carrying a machine gun.

One afternoon in 1954, as she was leaving the station, she was informed she had an important phone call. Hank Thompson, the number one country recording star in the nation, was on the other end. He had heard her on the radio and asked her to sing with his band, the Brazos Valley Boys at the Trianon Ball Room that Saturday night. Wanda was only fourteen years old and replied, "Mr. Thompson, I would love to, but I'll have to ask my mother."

The Trianon Ballroom, established by Bob Willis, was one of the finest dance halls in the Midwest. Wanda was a smashing hit and played several more times with Hank Thompson. He also helped her land a recording contract with Decca Records when she was sixteen. By the time she graduated high school she had a couple of hit songs and was ready to go on tour.

The first person she toured with was Elvis Presley, who was just getting started. She remembers meeting the good looking, 20-year-old, rock and roll singer who would become a legend in his time. He wore a bright yellow jacket. They toured together for two years and also dated. Wanda wore his class ring around her neck for a year. She and Elvis remained good friends for the rest of his life."

Elvis encouraged her to sing in the rockabilly style, which was becoming popular. By the end of the decade, Wanda had become one of America's first major female country and Rockabilly singers and was in demand for appearances all over the country.

Both her parents were supportive. Her father quit his job to travel with her and became her manager. Her mother made all her beautiful costumes. Wanda never moved to Nashville but kept Oklahoma City her headquarters.

Then, Wanda met the love of her life, Wendell

Goodman. They were married in 1961, and he took on the job of booking manager and tour manager. His parents also lived in Oklahoma City and the couple wanted to stay close to their families. Two children were born, Gina and Greg.

Wanda was nominated twice for a Grammy, and was a big attraction in Las Vegas for more that twelve years. In the seventies, she became a born-again Christian and switched to gospel ministry and music for fifteen years. Wanda sang and her husband gave his testimony. Those, she says, were fulfilling years.

In 1985, she was asked to go to Sweden to tour and record Rockabilly music. She toured Europe and Scandinavia four or five times a year and still does. She found that Rockabilly music is bigger now then ever before. In the last twenty years it has become popular all over the world. Few of its original singers, Elvis, Carl Perkins, Jerry Lee Lewis, Johnny Cash and Wanda are still alive.

Wanda has made between 50 and 60 albums, 8 tracks, cassettes and CDs around the world and has recorded in four languages.

For thirteen years, she returned to Maude each year for "Wanda Jackson Day." After a parade, car show, carnival, and a talent show, Wanda performed a concert in the evening. The money raised benefited the city by buying a fire truck, new paving, weapons and a car for the police department. These improvements also helped the citizens by lowering taxes. A room in the local museum is dedicated to Wanda and has many of her costumes, guitars, and photographs.

Wanda's top songs include, *Let's Have a Party, Right Or Wrong, A Little Bitty Tear Let Me Down, Silver Threads and Golden Needles*, and *Fujiyama Mama*, which was ranked number one in Japan. Wanda wrote many of the songs she recorded because there weren't many Rock and Roll songs written for females.

She has been inducted into many halls of fame, including the *Oklahoma Music Hall of Fame, The Oklahoma Country Hall of Fame*, and *the International Gospel Music Hall of Fame* and has been awarded the Oklahoma Native Daughter Award. Currently, there is an effort afoot to place her in the Rock and Roll Hall of Fame.

Wanda likes spending time with her family. Both her son and daughter live nearby and she has four grandchildren.

Today, Wanda is enjoying a resurgence in popularity as a new generation of fans has discovered her. She said she has more fans now than before and calls herself a rock and roll grandma.

Shannon Miller, America's Most Decorated gymnast.
Photo, Courtesy of Shannon Miller.

Shannon Miller

America's Most Decorated Gymnast

At the 1992 Summer Olympics, fifteen- year old Shannon Miller won five Olympic medals, more than any other American athlete. She received two silver medals for all around and balance beam, and three bronze for team, uneven bars and floor exercise. She's also the only U.S. woman to win two all-around titles at the World Gymnastics Championships (1993 and 1994.)

At the 1996 Olympic Games in Atlanta, Georgia, Shannon was on America's first ever gold medal team. She also received an individual gold medal for balance beam. She remains the most decorated American gymnast, winning more Olympic and World Championships medals than any other American gymnast, male or female, in history.

With the timing of a future gymnast, Shannon Lee Miller, was born in Rolla, Missouri, on March 10, 1977, the very day the doctor had predicted. The daughter of Ron and Claudia Miller, she joined two-year old Tessa in the family. Later a brother, Troy, was born.

When she was four months old, Shannon's pediatrician discovered a problem that would later make her astounding achievements more remarkable. Her legs turned in more than normal. For several months she wore specially designed baby shoes attached to a medal bar that turned her legs outward.

Her father, Ron accepted a position as a physics professor at the University of Central Oklahoma in Edmond when Shannon was six months old. Edmond is a quiet college town north of Oklahoma City. Claudia took a job as vice-president of a local bank.

Shannon's Olympic journey began in her own back yard when she was four. She begged her parents and Santa Claus for a trampoline for Christmas and got her wish. Although, on Christmas day the temperature outside was nine degrees, nothing would satisfy Shannon and Tessa until the trampoline was assembled. Shannon insisted that Santa would want her to play with it right away. Within two weeks, Shannon was doing front flips. Her parents decided that, before one of the girls was hurt they needed gymnastic lessons. They were enrolled at a local center called "Adventures in Gymnastics."

It was obvious, from the beginning, that Shannon had a talent. The coach recognized her potential and wanted her to take lessons every day for an hour. Her father began taking her back and forth to the gym on his lunch break. She was promoted to the junior elite program and within a year was able to keep up and surpass most of the other girls. Tessa excelled in many sports and liked to try new things. Shannon was focused on gymnastics.

Just before Shannon's ninth birthday, five girls from her gym accompanied by one parent each, and their coach attended a two week training camp in the Soviet Union. Claudia, who was by now, a gymnastic judge was invited to sit in on the training evaluation by the Soviet coaches. She was surprised to learn that out of forty gymnasts, the Russians picked three that they felt had potential. Shannon was one of the three.

While in Russia, Shannon met Soviet gymnast that she would later compete against and count as good friends. Also, in Russia, Shannon met another Oklahoman, gymnastics coach Steve Nunno, who was to play an important role in her life.

Steve was a former gymnast from New York, who paid his way through college on a gymnastic scholarship. He held a bachelors degree in business and a master's in sports administration. Steve coached a team called the Dynamos that trained at the Gymnastic Chalet, a gym owned by Bart Conner, a 1984 Olympic gold medalist, and Bart's coach, Paul Ziert.

Back home in the United States Shannon became even more serious about her sport. She switched gyms and began training with Steve in Norman, a 45 minute drive from Edmond. Her parents were beginning to realize the time and money commitment involved.

Shannon began competing in local class II competitions at the age of nine. Her first year was rocky. It seemed she fell at least once in every meet.

Under Steve's leadership, Shannon and her teammates progressed rapidly. Her first national competition was in 1987 at the University of Delaware in Newark. Although Shannon was the youngest member, she helped her team place third among some of the best clubs in the United States. This was her first television appearance and she received a lot of attention from the commentators who were impressed with her small size and her talent. They declared that in the future she would be one to watch.

Steve fulfilled his own dream and opened his own gym in Oklahoma City, which was closer for Shannon. She began training four hours a day, Monday through Saturday, taking Sunday to enjoy time with her family.

In June, 1988 Shannon placed second in the junior B division of the American Classic. A month later, she captured the national title in the 1988 U.S. Classic, establishing herself as the best gymnast in the country in the children's division. She was eleven years old.

Her next big win was the 1989 Junior Nationals, held at the United States Olympic Sports Festival in Oklahoma. Olympic sports taking place at the Festival included track and field, diving, swimming, basketball, tennis, volleyball and gymnastics. She was the tiniest contestant weighing in at fifty-five pounds. For the first time, Oklahoma fans began to take notice as they watched either at the event or on television. Their newest hometown star won the bronze medal in the all around competition and the gold medal on uneven bars.

On November 8 Shannon appeared in the 1989 Tour of Champions exhibition, in Oklahoma City. Few people knew that Shannon had badly injured her hamstring in the spring of 1989 but had competed with the injury for six more months. Now the doctor insisted she take four months off. While she didn't cease training, she did have to cut back considerably.

Shannon entered the 1990 U.S. Championships as a senior even though she was only thirteen. She was the youngest competitor ever to make the senior national team. The Press nicknamed her "Mighty Mite Miller".

At fourteen she became the youngest gymnast ever to win a medal at the 1991 World Championships. At four feet six inches tall and 69 pounds, she was the smallest member of the U.S. National Team. For the first time the American team captured the silver medal. Shannon was ranked third in the nation and sixth in the world.

Shannon did not care for publicity, even though she became one of the most sought after sports figures. Her low voice and quiet personality made reporters describe her as shy. She was once described in an *International Gymnast* magazine article as "speaking softly and carrying big tricks."

Shannon began looking toward the 1992 Olympics in Barcelona, Spain. Her goal for 1992 was to win the U.S. Championship and the Olympic trials. Hopefully she would go to the Olympics and maybe bring home a medal. Most Olympic hopefuls took a year away from school. Steve wanted Shannon to drop out but She refused. A ninth grader at Edmond North High School she continued classes, maintained a 4.0 grade point average and was a member of the Oklahoma and the National Honor Society's.

Her daily routine was to wake up at 6:00 a.m., go to Dynamo Gym in Edmond where she did stretching and strength exercises, worked out, and practiced dance routines until 8:30. Then, after attending class all day, it was back to the gym for five more hours of work. Practice ended about 9:00 p.m., then it was home, for dinner, homework, and bed around 11:00 p.m.

Unfortunately at the end of March, before the summer Olympics, Shannon fell and dislocated her left elbow. After a difficult decision whether to put a cast on her arm or to perform surgery, Shannon agreed to the surgery to insert a pin. This was followed by extensive physical therapy. Nationals were only three weeks away and the Olympic Trials were only seven weeks ahead. Shannon sat out of workouts for only one day. Even if she could not use her arm, she would go through the routines and do some one- arm tumbling. With the Olympics only three months away, the injury just made her more determined to compete and to win.

Shannon flew to Baltimore for the 1992 Olympic trials on Thursday, June 11. Although it was only two months after her surgery, she finished first. The U.S. team consisted of Shannon, Kim Zmeskal, Kerri Strug, Betty Okino, Dominique Dawes, Michelle Campi, and Wendy Bruce.

At 15, Shannon was one of the youngest athletes in Barcelona. On the second day of the Olympics she was awarded a 9.95, the highest score of the United States team. She received five medals, the silver all-around, a silver for balance beam and bronze on floor exercise, bronze on uneven bars, and a team bronze. By winning the most medals of any U.S. athlete in Barcelona, she became the most decorated American at the 1992 Olympics, both summer and winter. Her five medals were also the most ever won in a non-boycotted Olympics. Mary Lou Retton won five medals in the 1984 Los Angeles Olympics but the games were boycotted by the Soviet Union.

Fame changed life for Shannon. When she arrived home in Oklahoma City, her plane was met by hundreds of fans. (My daughters and I were in that mob of well wishers). A parade was held in her hometown of Edmond and Shannon Miller Parkway was named for her. Signs were erected at the city boundaries whch read "City of Edmond, home of Shannon Miller, winner of five Olympic medals, Barcelona, 1992". She was given a car although she was too young to drive.

Governor David Walters declared Shannon Miller Appreciation Day in Oklahoma and honored the 15 year old with a special proclamation. She was named honorary Governor of Oklahoma and honorary Mayor of Oklahoma City.

Shannon had a good year in 1993, winning one award after another. In January, she made history by becoming the youngest person ever named Sports Headliner by the Oklahoma March of Dimes Sports Headliner Committee. She was named Female Athlete of the Year at the National Athletic Awards in Detroit, in February.

Shannon celebrated her Sweet Sixteen Birthday party in March with pizza, go-carts, and a slumber party. Her mother said it was the first birthday celebration for Shannon since her ninth birthday.

In April, she won a gold medal in the all-around competition in the World Gymnastic Championships in Birmingham, England.

She was named the Sports Woman of the month in both April and May by the U.S. Olympic Committee.

In July, she won the gold medal for the all-around competition at the U.S. Olympic Festival in San Antonio and in August the title at the National Gymnastics Championships in Salt Lake City.

In April of 1994, Shannon won her second consecutive all-around title at the World Gymnastics Championships in Australia, making her the first American gymnast to take the back-to-back honor. A different honor was bestowed on her in 1995 when she graduated with honors from Edmond North High School.

But, Shannon wasn't finished yet. She had not won an Olympic gold medal and she wanted one badly. She went to the 1996 Olympics in Atlanta and led her "Team USA" to its first team gold medal. The team was named the Magnificent Seven and performed in a dramatic made- for- television showdown among the worlds best. Shannon delivered an almost perfect balance beam performance, winning the gold medal before a cheering 32,000 fans at the Georgia Dome. She was the first American to ever win gold on the balance beam.

She returned home from Atlanta with a celebrity status of legendary proportions. Balloons, roses, banners, and a parade again welcomed her back to Oklahoma. She received many endorsement offers and left Atlanta with a new agent and business deals in the works. She and her teammates graced the famous orange box of Wheaties and appeared in a television commercial for the breakfast food; "Eat your Wheaties, We did." The team traveled across the country in the John Hancock Tour. Her agent reported that the cost of having Shannon appear at an event ranged from $5,000 to $50,000 depending on what she was expected to do. Sometimes she signed autograph, sometimes, she made an appearance, or she could be the featured speaker at an event. Shannon also became involved in charity work. Since Barcelona, she had her own line of workout wear, the Shannon Miller Workout Collection by Elite Sportswear.

After the John Hancock tour, Shannon enrolled as a full time student at the University of Oklahoma. Mutual friends introduced her to O.U. medical student Chris Phillips. A year later Chris proposed through a fortune cookie at a Chinese restraint.

A gold medal event happened in June of 1999 when Shannon married Oklahoma native Chris Philllips, a medical student, before 900 guests. Twenty four people in the wedding party had 11 Olympic medals between them, not counting the bride who has seven of her own. Among her bridemaids were the other members of the Magnificent Seven; Amanda Borden, Dominique Dawes, Amy Chow, Jaycie Phelps, Dominique Moceanu, and Kerri Strug. The other six Bridesmaids were Kim Zmeskal, Dynamo teammates Jennie Thompson, Heather Brink, and Soni Meduna, Dynamo coach Peggy Liddick and tutor Terri Thomas. Tessa Miller,

Shannon's sister was the maid of honor. Olympic champion Bart Conner was one of the groomsmen. Among the guest was Bart Connor's wife and Olympic gold medalist, Nadia Comaneci, the darling of the 1976 Olympics. The wedding was covered on Extra and People magazine. However, Shannon filed for divorce in 2004, which was final in 2006.

A sculpture of Shannon by Shan Gray was erected in Shannon Miller Park in Edmond and remains as an inspiration to all young gymnasts.

Shannon's medal count is awesome; Seven Olympic medals, and nine World Championship medals since 1992. She has won 58 International and 49 National competition medals and more than 50 percent are gold and all before the age of nineteen.

At 20, she won the University Games in Italy, bringing her international count to 59. In 2002 she won silver on the uneven bars at the U.S. Championships, bringing her count to 50 medals in national competitions.

In 2003, Shannon received her BBA degree from the University of Houston and is pursuing a law degree at Boston College. She visits Oklahoma frequently.

She was inducted into the U.S. Gymnastic Hall of Fame in 2003 and in October 2005 was named to the class of 2006 inductees to the U.S. Olympic Hall of Fame. Also in the spring of 2006, Shannon was inducted into the International Gymnastic Hall of Fame.

She continues to be active in the gymnastic world as a television commentator, clinic coach, performer, and motivational speaker.

Wilma Mankiller, Chief of the Cherokee Nation. Photo, Courtesy of Wilma Mankiller.

Wilma Mankiller

Chief of the Cherokee Nation

A native of Mankiller Flats, near Stillwell, Wilma Mankiller made history in 1987, when she was elected the first female principal chief of the Cherokee Nation. As the Cherokee leader, she represented the second-largest tribe in the United States. She was awarded the Presidential Medal of Freedom from President Clinton in 1998.

"Mankiller" is an ancient Cherokee military title, bestowed on a warrior, in the position of safeguarding a village. The name is fitting for a woman who protected not just her village but a nation.

November 18, 1945, Wilma Pearl Mankiller was born the fifth in a family of eleven children. Her father Charlie was a full-blooded Cherokee, and her mother Irene was Dutch Irish.

Wilma always knew she had come from a proud and courageous people. As a child she had heard stories of the forced removal of her people from Southeastern United States to Indian Territory, later known as Oklahoma, the land of the red man. Wilma's ancestors made the 1200-mile exodus, known as The Trail of Tears in the winter of 1838-39. Some eighteen thousand people, nearly one fourth of the Cherokees who made the journey, died along the way. The Mankillers survived.

Tales, passed down from relatives, told how their people had left behind their homes, farms and all their belongings. But the Cherokee Nation reestablished its government, schools, and culture in Indian Territory.

In 1907, upon statehood, the federal government dismantled the tribal government and divided up the commonly held land into individual allotments of 160 acres. Wilma's grandfather John Mankiller was given an allotment, which passed down to her father Charlie and her aunt Sally Leach. Those woodsy hills near Stillwell were named "Mankiller Flats.

Wilma's family didn't have indoor plumbing or electricity. Wilma and her siblings hauled water a quarter mile to the house. What they ate, they usually grew, fished or hunted. The children contributed to the family income by picking beans or strawberries, or cutting wood for railroad ties.

In her book, *Every Day is a Good Day: Reflections by Contemporary Indigenous Women,* Wilma tells of her childhood experiences.

> Then there were the 'bless-your-little-heart' ladies. They were white Christian women who made our family one of their charities by bringing used clothing and other gifts to our small wood frame home. When I saw their big car approaching our house, I ran and hid. While walking to and from school, they would sometimes stop and offer us a ride, murmuring, "Bless your little hearts." I understood that these women thought they were better than us and that they would accept us if only we were more like them.

> Many years later, a white woman raising money to give scholarships to indigenous students told me she wanted to give "pride back to the Indians." She had such a staggering sense

of entitlement; she didn't know the highly in-
sulting and patronizing nature of that statement. She reminded me of the "bless-your-
little-heart" ladies from my childhood.

When Wilma was twelve her family was again
uprooted by a federal program designed to urban-
ize rural Indians. The Bureau of Indian Affairs Relo-
cation Program promised the family a better life.
They were sent from the Oklahoma countryside to
a poverty-stricken, high crime neighborhood in San
Francisco. This was as much a cultural shock as her
ancestors had experienced in 1839.

The Mankiller family was squeezed into an
apartment in Hunters Point, a housing project, in a
city where employment for Native Americans was
scarce, if at all. Her father worked on the docks and
the warehouses along the wharf. He was active in
the community.

Wilma studied sociology at San Francisco
State University. Just before her eighteenth birthday,
she married a wealthy Ecuadorian student. Assum-
ing the expected role of housewife, she had two
daughters, Felicia born in 1964 and Gina in 1966.

Her husband wanted a traditional wife and
although Wilma tried to fit into that picture, she was
becoming more involved in the world around her.
In the late 1960's, San Francisco was an exciting
place full of social unrest. Wilma's concern for Native American issues was ignited in 1969, when a
band of university students occupied the former
prison at Alcatraz. They were there for nineteen
months bringing public attention to the problems
of Native Americans.

"Those college students who participated in
Alcatraz articulated a lot of feelings I had that I'd
never been able to express," Wilma told John Hughes

in an interview for the *Chicago Tribune* (May 14, 1986). "I was a mother, so I couldn't join them, but I did fund-raising and got involved in the activist movement."

Wilma began attending college at night at San Francisco State University. She worked for the Native American programs coordinator for the Oakland, California public school system. She was also involved with volunteer work among Indians in the Bay area. Learning about tribal governance and its history compelled her to take a fresh look at the Cherokee experience; she saw the trail of broken promises and the years of injustice to her people. She has said many times that the activist Wilma Mankiller, of that time, could never have become chief of the Cherokee Nation.

During the Alcatraz occupation, both Wilma and her father were diagnosed with polycystic kidney disease. Charlie Mankiller, died in 1971.

Wanting more involvement with her people, Wilma divorced her husband, in 1976, after ten years of marriage. The single mother and her two young daughters returned to Oklahoma. She was knowledgeable about land and treaty rights, skilled in grant writing and was filled with faith for her people.

Wilma went to work for the Cherokee Nation as an economic coordinator while attending school for community planning at the University of Arkansas. She saw her people's overwhelming need for adequate housing, employment, education and health care. She worked hard obtaining grant money and initiating services, but she was still angry.

In many interviews, Wilma has said, what changed her, was a 1979 tragic automobile accident that killed a close friend and badly injured her. The wreck left Wilma's legs splintered, her ribs broken and her face crushed. Her body was so mangled that emergency technicians could not determine her sex. The head on collision occurred when Wilma, traveling alone, crested a hill, and was hit by her friend, the other driver, who was passing two slower cars and was in Wilma's lane of traffic.

Wilma spent eight weeks in the hospital in Fort Smith where many surgeries were performed to put her face and shattered bones back together. Before it was over she endured 17 operations most of which were on her right leg. Doctors discussed amputating the leg and worried that she would never walk again.

During the healing process, Wilma adopted what she has called "a Cherokee approach" to life – what the elder's call "being of good mind." It means to think positively, to take what has been handed out and turn it into a better path.

Recovery from the wreck was slow and painful. Then in November, 1980, she was diagnosed with myasthenia gravis, a chronic neuromuscular disease that causes weakness in the voluntary muscles of the body. Treatment included surgery on her thymus, followed by steroid therapy.

A few weeks later she was back on the job with new enthusiasm. She now realized how precious life was. In 1981, she founded, and was named the director of, the Cherokee Nation Community Development Department. She obtained funding and spearheaded an ambitious project called the Bell Community Revitalization Project. With money from the federal government, private funds and their own labor, the residents of the tiny community of Bell remodeled dilapidated housing, constructed new homes, and laid their own 26 mile line that brought running water to their homes for the first time. In addition to making the physical improvements, the residents developed a strong bond and a sense of control over their lives.

The project brought national attention and became a model for other Native American communities. It also established Wilma as an expert in community development and brought her to the attention of the tribal leaders.

Ross Swimmer, principal chief of the Cherokee Nation, enlisted her to run as his deputy chief in the next election. Swimmer was a conservative Republican, and Wilma was a liberal Democrat, but both were committed to rebuilding the Nation.

She was not prepared for the tough criticism she encountered because she was a female. This was the first time, Wilma encountered overt sexism. Her tires were slashed and her family endured death threats. She decided early she didn't have time to defend herself as to whether gender had any thing to do with leadership. More important issues needed to be discussed.

The two narrowly won the election, and Wilma became the first woman deputy principal chief. Swimmer resigned in 1985 to head the Bureau of Indian Affairs in Washington. Wilma stepped into the job he left behind - principal chief – another first for a Cherokee woman.

In 1986, Wilma married her old friend, Charlie Soap, a full blooded Cherokee and the former director of the tribal development program. The couple met when they worked together on the Bell project.

Then, in 1987, Wilma won a full four-year term, becoming the first woman elected chief of a major American Indian group. As principal chief she managed 1,000 tribal government employees and a budget of $47 million for the 78,000 member Cherokee nation in Oklahoma. The job was much like being the chief executive officer of a large corporation, a government official and a social worker all at the same time. She also spent a lot of time advocating the needs of the tribe on the state level and in Washington, D.C.

No one expected the national impact her election created. In her unique position she has been able to bring attention to the rights of American Indians and share the story of the Cherokee Nation with the rest of the world.

Newsweek named her to its list of heroes, and *Ladies Home Journal* called her one of the most important women in America. *Ms.* magazine chose her as one of their 1987 Women of the Year. In 1986, she was named to the Oklahoma Women's Hall of Fame. That same year, she received a citation for Outstanding Contributions to American Leadership and Native American Culture from the Harvard Foundation. In 1988, she was awarded the John W. Gardner Leadership Award by Independent Sector, a non-profit coalition of 659 national voluntary organizations, foundations and corporations with a national interest in philanthropy. She was cited as a "builder of people and of causes."

She received the highest civilian honor the United States bestows when, in 1989, President Bill Clinton presented her with the Presidential Medal of Freedom. The award recognizes exceptional meritorious service.

Two years after her election, Wilma's old kidney problems reappeared, and she needed a transplant. Her brother, Don, donated one of his kidneys. The surgery was successful, and Wilma returned to work within three weeks.

After many family consultations, she decided to run again in 1991. Many things remained that she wanted to accomplish. She was elected to another four year term by 83% of the vote. By this time the Cherokees believed it was safe to have a woman as chief. She had become an example of strong female leadership for the whole country.

Wilma's terms in office produced enormous results for her people: health clinics, a hospital, Cherokee business enterprises and numerous self-help initiatives. She developed a Department of Commerce, which combined all the tribe business enterprises including a motel, restaurant and a gift shop. A $12 million job corp center was built in Tahlequah during her term.

From 1986 to 1994, the population of the Cherokee Nation grew from 55,000 to 156,000, and the annual budget nearly doubled, to $86 million from $44 million.

Saying it was time for a change for herself and the Cherokee Nation, Wilma announced in 1994 that she would not run for reelection. Later, she admitted that her health was also a factor. She had been principal chief for a decade.

Kidney failure made it necessary, in 1996, for her to endure another transplant. This time, her niece, Virlee Williamson, was the donor. A few weeks shy of completing a Montgomery fellowship at Dartmouth College in Hanover, New Hampshire, Wilma was admitted to the hospital in Boston when she failed to improve from a bout with pneumonia. Doctors discovered Lymphoma. Kidney and heart transplant patients are more prone to get lymphoma because of their weakened immune system. She received chemotherapy and once again her strong spirit refused to give up.

An accomplished writer, she had co-authored in 1993, with Michael Wallis, the best selling auto-biography, *Mankilller, A Chief and her People*. In 2004, she wrote, *Every Day is a Good Day*, in which she featured articles by Native American women friends

---

addressing issues specific to their culture.

A highly sought-after speaker, Wilma has delivered more than 100 lectures on the challenges facing Native Americans and Women in the 21st century. She serves on the board of the Freedom Forum and the Ford Foundation, and is a member of the external Diversity Advisory Council for Merrill Lynch.

Wilma told Melissa Howell, in a 2006 article for the *Oklahoman* that she "enjoys life to the fullest, reading, writing, serving on foundation boards and being a guest speaker and professor."

Most of all she enjoys her family. Her two daughters, Charlie's sons, their ten grandchildren, her mother, and numerous other relatives live near Wilma and Charlie's home at Mankiller Flats.

Though no longer in office, Wilma Mankiller remains the most celebrated Cherokee of the 21st. century.

Leona Mitchell – Oklahoma's most famous opera singer.
Photo, Courtesy of Leona Mitchell.

Leona Mitchell

Internationally Renown Operatic Soprano

Enid, Oklahoma, may be a town better known for producing wheat, poultry, and oil than opera singers; however, Leona Mitchell rose from singing in the choir of her father's small church in Enid to becoming one of the best known opera stars in the world. A favorite of New York's Metropolitan Opera, she has performed for the most prestigious companies.

Leona, the daughter of a preacher and a nurse, was the tenth of fifteen children born to Doctor's Hulon and Pearl Mitchell. She grew up in a home filled with music; her father played many instruments, her mother was a pianist, and all fifteen children sang or performed in some way. For many years they were billed as The Musical Mitchell's with different family members involved at various times. During the 1950s Reverend Mitchell also worked as host and disk jockey of a Christian music show on KCRC Radio. Leona inherited the family's musical gifts, played the violin, and sang in the Antioch Church choir. Her older siblings teased her, saying that she couldn't sing. She cried and thought, *I'll show them.*

Leona learned music by ear and for many years did not know that notes could be read. As a senior in high school, she learned an aria from Aida by rote and with the help of her high school teacher, Maurine Priebe.

To please a teacher, she auditioned for the music department at Oklahoma City University. To her surprise she received a full scholarship. There she studied with internationally recognized voice teacher, Inez Silberg.

In a 1982 interview in *Time Magazine* Leona said, "I thought Moon River was serious music. Honey, when you're from Enid, you hardly ever hear of opera."

In her freshman year at Oklahoma City University, she played in *The Story of Ruth*, the first opera she had ever seen. By the end of her senior year, she had sung in twelve student productions and won 35 vocal contests. Leona received her B.A. in music from Oklahoma University in 1971.

Shortly after graduation, she took first place in the prestigious Merola Opera Program competition in San Francisco.

Her Merola victory in 1971 brought her a summer apprenticeship in the San Francisco Opera. Two years later, she sang Micaela in Bizet's *Carmen* at the San Francisco Spring Opera Theater.

In 1974, she won a $10,000 Opera America grant, and moved to Los Angeles to study with her mentor and voice teacher Ernes St. John Metz. In the mid-1970s, Leona launched what would become a spectacular career.

She made her Metropolitan Opera debut in 1975 as Micaela in *Carmen,* this time opposite Tenor Placido Domingo's Don Jose. The critics received her warmly, called it a sensational performance, and praised her fresh voice and winning demeanor.

The Met invited her back immediately to perform in Mozart's *The Magic Flute* and Puccini's *La Boheme.*

The role of Bess in Gershwin's immortal *Porgy and Bess* catapulted Leona to international fame. She sang with the Cleveland Orchestra for the London Records complete recording of the opera.

According to the *New York Post*, "In just a few years, Leona had risen to one of the most impressive lyric sopranos today." She received critical praise both in the United States and abroad and established herself as one of the leading stars of the New York Met, and the San Francisco, Paris, and Australia Operas. She appeared in such roles as Liu, Pamima, Mimi, Micaela, Mme. Lidoine, Madame Butterfly, Manon Lescaut, Aida, and Ballo Trovafore.

She also sang with major symphony orchestras of the world in Los Angeles, New York, Boston, Philadelphia, Pittsburgh, London, San Francisco, and Cleveland.

In 1983, she shared the stage at the Met with world renown Luciano Pavarotti in Verdi's *Erani*. That same year she was inducted into the Oklahoma Hall of Fame.

Leona's sister, Barbara Finley of Enid, said, "Leona was always generous with her family, often taking along a sister, or a niece or nephew on these incredible trips. Many of her relatives had experiences they could only dream about. This was also good for Leona, because in the early years it was a little frightening to travel alone, for a young woman who had never been outside Enid, Oklahoma."

Upon meeting Leona, I was struck by her beauty. Opera singers are often stereotyped as heavy-set. Leona is petite with a lovely smile. Outgoing and friendly, she posed for a picture, even though she laughed that she wore jeans.

Leona holds honorary doctorate degrees from both Oklahoma City University and the University of Oklahoma.

She was recognized by a joint session of the Oklahoma Legislature, Governor George Nigh, the Black Legislative Caucus, and the Arts Council of Oklahoma in 1985. She also served as designated honorary chairman of Black Heritage Month in her home state.

Leona has appeared with the Tulsa Opera and opened the Central Oklahoma Series at the University of Central Oklahoma. In 1992, she returned to her alma mater, OCU, to inaugurate the new Petree Recital Hall.

Her beautiful voice and commanding presence have led to frequent television appearances both in the United States and abroad. Her performances have been telecast on PBS's *Live from the Met*. She was seen coast-to-coast on the Gala Statue of Liberty Concert *Live from Central Park* on ABC-TV. She performed with Zubin Mehta and the New York Philharmonic, the Kennedy Center Honors Program and the PBS *Live from Lincoln Center* series with Luciano Pavarotti.

In addition Leona was a guest on the *Dick Cavett Show*, the *Merv Griffin Show*, the CBS *Good Morning Program* and Jerry Lewis's *Muscular Dystrophy Telethon*.

In 2001, Leona was inducted into the Oklahoma Music Hall of Fame. The only opera star in the prestigious Hall. Other women inductees include Patti Page, Wanda Jackson, and Kay Starr.

Leona has donated many of her costumes, programs and memorabilia to the Southern Heights Heritage Center and Museum in Enid. Her sister Barbara and niece Angela Molette have opened the museum in their father's old church, The Antioch Church of God in Christ. It was their father's hope that this building would serve as an educational resource center for the black community. That dream was realized in 2002, when the museum was opened a year after his death. A room reconstructed as a dressing room contains gowns and posters donated by Leona.

Leona's wedding dress, cake topper, program and other mementoes are also displayed. She was married to Elmer Coles Bush III, October 20, 1979, at the chic, historic Grace Cathedral on San Francisco's Nob Hill. Ten bridesmaids and ten groomsmen were in attendance. The reception was hosted at the home of billionaires Gordon P. and Ann Getty.

Elmer had taught in Los Angeles and was also an outstanding musician, a former member of the Albert McNeil Jubilee Singers. He traveled the world singing with this renowned chorale ensemble. Since their marriage he serves as Leona's manager. They have a twenty-one year old son, Elmer Bush IV. Leona and Elmer live in Houston, but spent a considerable amount of time in Enid with Leona's eighty-nine-year old mother, Pearl who died in 2006. Pearl was a delightful storyteller gifted with a good memory. She helped the museum and with recording the local history.

Leona's contributions to Oklahoma made her the special guest performer for the opening of the new history center in Oklahoma City in November of 2005.

Just a few days later, she spent Thanksgiving back on Broadway, only this time on the *Oklahoma Rising* float in New York City's 79th annual Macy's Thanksgiving Day Parade. The float commemorates Oklahoma's upcoming anniversary of 100 years of statehood. Joining her on the Centennial float were other Oklahoma notables including actress Kristin Chenoweth, baseball greats Bobby Mercer and Johnny Bench, Olympic gymnast Shannon Miller, former football coach Barry Switzer, Choctaw Nation representative Gena Timberman Howard and singer song-writer Jimmy Webb.

Merline Lovelace

Woman in Command

After a 23-year career in the United States Air Force, serving tours of duty in Vietnam, the Pentagon, and as commander of Elgin Air Force Base, Colonel Merline Lovelace launched a second career as a writer, basing many of her tales on her own experiences in uniform. Since then she's published more than 65 novels making her one of the most read romance authors in America.

Plaques and photographs covered the walls of Merline Lovelace's home office. Some were from the military, others recognition of her writing. She laughed, "There are many more in the attic. My husband, Al, is also a retired air force colonel, so between the two of us we have quite a collection."

Military life came naturally to Merline. Her father served in the European Theater in World War II and retired as Master Sergeant from the Air Force in 1961. Merlin married Alyce Thomas the day after the Pearl Harbor invasion. Their life together was spent at one military base after another. Merline's mother was a real trooper packing up kids, dogs, cats, turtles, and parakeets to move across the country.

Merline was born at Northampton, Massachusetts. As a military brat she lived in about half the states and Newfoundland and spent three years in France. She loved the travel and meeting new people. Her mother always made each move an adventure. She encouraged reading and books were Merline's constant companions.

Merline Lovelace, Air Force Colonel and romance writer. Photo, Courtesy of Merline Lovelace.

The children were all influenced by military life. One brother and one sister served in the Marines, another sister and Merline served in the Air Force.

After high school, Merline attended Ripon College, a small liberal arts school in Wisconsin, where she majored in German and Russian. Her junior year she was selected to attend a special language program at Princeton University. She studied Mandarin Chinese there and at Middlebury College in Vermont. At Middlebury the students were not permitted to speak English. Merline is fluent in Chinese, speaks French and German, and is knowledgeable in Latin and Greek. Her skill with languages was helpful in the military and also as a writer.

She seemed to be heading toward a career in the state department. After she graduated from college she was accepted into a Ph.D. program at the University of Michigan. Her trunks had already been shipped when she sat beside an Air Force recruiter at the lunch counter in a Rexall Drug Store. The recruiter persuaded her to join the Air Force.

She told him, "I'm supposed to leave for Michigan on Friday. If you can get me signed up before then, I'll join." By Friday, she was a member of the United States Air Force and has never regretted it.

Similar to one of her romance novels, on her second day at her first duty station, Merline met a dashing young captain, named Al Lovelace. They were stationed at Randolph Air Force Base in San Antonio when they began dating. Then, she received orders to Taiwan. Al flew over to see her a few times. Merline said, "Long distance romance was for the birds."

They were married in Taiwan and honeymooned in Hong Kong. "My husband is the hero in every single one of my books," Merline revealed.

Seven months later she was stationed back in the States, at Carswell Air Force Base in Fort Worth. A year later, Al received orders to Vietnam, and Merline immediately volunteered to go also. Family members were not assigned to the same unit in a war zone, so Al served at DaNang, while Merline was at Tan Son Nhut in Saigon. They were there during the Easter Offensive of '72. It was not an experience she would like to repeat, but it gave fodder to her book *Duty and Dishonor*.

Vietnam was interesting to Merline. She found the people fascinating, the country tragic and ripped apart by war. Each female officer was assigned a sponsor, and they all lived together in a two-story barracks.

Many plum assignments followed –Eglin AFB, Florida; Maxwell AFB, Alabama; Kirktland AFB, New Mexico; and Randolph AFB, Texas. Merline would recommend the military to any young men or woman who loves adventure and being part of something important.

Spending time at the Pentagon was like procuring a masters degree in politics. She worked for the Assistant Secretary of the Air Force and was there during the Panama crisis, the invasion of Grenada and the presidential transition from Carter to Regan.

Serving as Support Wing Commander of Eglin Air Force Base was her favorite and most demanding assignment. Running an air force base was like being mayor of a small city, with its own hospital, fire department, police, transportation and housing departments, and 2000 troops under her direction. About 20,000 troops and civilians worked on the base. Merline cut ribbons for new buildings, spoke at community events, investigated airplane crashes, one murder, and all the things a chief executive does in a small city. In addition, she operated the airfield, the communications tower, and served as a landlord to other flying units on the base. Always, on call, it was a 24 hour a day, seven days a week job. This became the theme of her book, *Line of Duty*.

Al retired in 1988 and became "the commander's wife." A strong and secure person, Al didn't mind. Married 36 years, the couple feels fortunate they were able to share their experiences.

Merline retired in 1991. Always a book lover and having worked in libraries while in school, she considered opening a bookstore. Not wanting to be tied down to that schedule, she tried her hand at writing. What better thing to write about than what she knew best – military life. She also chose romance novels. "They have a powerful message of love and hope."

Her first book, *Bits and Pieces* was a contemporary romance, set at Eglin, the base she formerly commanded. The book was an immediate success. First published in 1993, it was reprinted in 2005. *Maggie and the Colonel* was also set at Eglin.

Since then she has written 70 books, 65 are published and the rest are in the pipeline.. She completes more than four manuscripts a year and loves every minute of it. Twenty-three years of military life have made her a disciplined person. When working on a novel, she does a lot of up-front work. Big notebooks are kept for each novel, containing a detailed outline for each chapter, the setting, the plot, and a description of the characters. When she sits down to write, most of the hard work has been done. She writes fast and tight. Seldom does she do much revision. Writing is a full time job. She works from early morning until mid-afternoon on the current book. The afternoon is devoted to the business angle

– writing proposals, answering fan mail, scheduling, and promoting the novels. Usually, three books are in progress, the one she is writing, one she is revising, and one she is pitching to publishers.

Upon completion of each book, she gives herself a month off. A ritual always performed in the cleansing of the office. While she is working, the room becomes messy, but when a book is finished, the area gets a thorough sweep. Then she and Al usually go on an informative, romantic trip.

Ideas are all around her. Merline keeps an idea file and a file of brochures of places she has visited, not only for descriptions but also as potential settings for future books.

Romance novels have become more sophisticated in the last few years, now often referred to as "woman's fiction." Merline believes in the romance genre the primary focus is on relationships as well as suspense, mystery and tension. In broader women's fiction, the emphasis may be more on an action line or relationship that is not necessarily male and female, such as a mother and daughter relationship. She laughs, "In a romance you are going to get a good story and good sex."

Although she is sometimes referred to as a woman's fiction writer, and is a member of the International Thriller Writers Association, she thinks of herself more as a romance writer. She says, "I might write mystery or suspense, but I've got to have that man-woman relationship. I have to have a happy ending."

Merline also writes a series of books set in Oklahoma. Carefully researched, with all the biographies and maps filed in her notebook, these books are popular. She likes to alternate between histories and contemporaries because it allows her to use different voices and styles. Contemporaries are faster paced, she says, and histories allow more time for exploration. She likes to tell the reader something, whether it's historical fact or information about a government agency.

Living in Oklahoma is "perfect" for this prolific author. For a short time after retirement they lived in Albuquerque. Then decided to move to Oklahoma City as Al's family lived in the area and Merline had become friends with local romance authors.

"Oklahoma romance writers are the most sharing, caring people on earth," she says. "Attending writer's workshops and conferences is very important, not only to hone the craft but also for the socialization. Writing is a very solitary profession, and you need that communication with others."
Now, Merline is most often a speaker at these meetings. She feels a responsibility to share her knowledge with new writers.

The University of Oklahoma recognized Merline as the Oklahoma Writer of the Year in 1998. She received the Rita Award for the 2001 best novella by the Romance Writers of America and the Reviewers Choice Award by Romantic Times Magazine in 1993 and 2002.

Ida "B." Blackburn, television pioneer, with John Wayne. Photo Courtesy of Ida "B."

Ida Mae Blackburn

Television Pioneer Ida "B"

Ida Blackburn began a 43-year career in Okla-homa television in 1958, as nationally syndicated Romper Room teacher, "Miss Ida". One of the early pioneers of live television programming, her " Ida B show" became one of the most watched shows on tele-vision.

The year, 1929, was not a good year for much of America as banks closed and the stock market crashed. But, it was a good year for the nine members of the Turley family in Ninnekah, Oklahoma as they welcomed their newest member, Ida Mae.

The child's father said she was a bit of an exhibitionist and was destined to a career of public exposure.

When Ida was five years old the family moved to Chickasha, where her father worked in the gas fields. She entered school, but at the age of six, was stricken with polio and not expected to live. In less than a year, however, she recovered and learned to walk again.

The family moved to Chandler when Ida was fifteen years old. There, she was the lead singer in the glee club, starred in school operettas and was a cheerleader during her junior and senior years. In the twelfth grade she was voted band queen. After her graduation, the family moved back to Chickasha, where Ida attended the Oklahoma College for Women.

After one year at OCW, she transferred to Central State University in Edmond, where she headed the drama club and starred in many of the college productions. She received her degree in music from Central State and taught music in Choctaw and Arcadia High Schools. She later served as Minister of Music at Wesley United Methodist Church in El Reno.

Ida was married her senior year in college. During her teaching years two children were born, Bobby in 1951, and Betty in 1953.

In the 1950s, Ida's father suffered with emphysema and spent a great deal of time watching television. He was convinced that Ida should be on TV.

Three months after his death, in 1957, Ida saw a commercial advertising for schoolteachers between ages 21-28 for a nationally syndicated show. She was not only a teacher, but a music teacher and she was 28 years old. She remembered her dad's belief that television was her destiny.

She auditioned for and was selected as the Romper Room teacher on KOCO-TV. She was sent to Baltimore, Maryland for two weeks of training. A naïve Ida had never been on an airplane, a train, or in a big city. She wore a hat and white gloves and carried lots of luggage. She registered in an old hotel in a bad part of town. Each night, she slept with a chair propped against the door.

The training consisted of learning the philosophy of communicating with children and a live audience. This experience served as a foundation for her later work. Television stations across the country each had their own Miss Mary or Miss Betty or Miss Ida. Viewers recall Miss Ida holding up a mirror with the frame cut out chanting, "Romper bomper stomper boo, tell me, tell me, do. Magic mirror tell me today, did all my friends have fun at play?"

Back home, Channel 5's tower was at Crescent and the license was for the town of Enid. This was the first programming filmed from the Oklahoma City satellite studio. The station itself was an old grocery store on Britton Road, one block east of Western. A curtain separated the studio from the rest of the office. Only one camera was used. *Romper Room* was filmed, as was everything in those days, in black and white. Ida earned $60 a week.

The studio was so small that when the five children appeared on the show, they sat around a table, then later rode their stick horses around that same table. When the show came on at ten o'clock in the morning, the staff went for coffee and took their phones off the hook, as there simply wasn't room for everyone.

After a year, the show's production moved to Enid. Ida didn't want to relocate so Carol Arnold, later featured on KTOK radio, replaced her.

Ida had one year left on her contract with *Romper Room* syndication and was not allowed to do any on-air television for a year. Nor was she allowed to use the name Miss Ida. She convinced The Dennis Donuts Company to hire her as "Ida Blackburn, the Donut Girl". As public relations manager she helped open four outlets and worked promotionally with children in the schools. Parents would call into KTOK radio and vote for their favorite teacher, and Ida would personally deliver a basket of apples for the teacher and Dennis Donuts for the children.

She wanted to return to television and designed a show, which she convinced Channel Five to try. She copied categories of interest from the editorial page of a *Ladies Home Journal,* and formatted a show around those features. This served as a forerunner for today's magazine shows.

She originated a combination mother and children's show, on which children's cartoons were shown. Then Ida went live with tips on fashion, exercise and community events. The show premiered in 1960, and was called, *At home with Ida B.* She made $100 a week until 1975.

In her first promo picture, Ida wore a short western dress, had her hair styled in a wave, and held a teacup in her hand. Her first celebrity guest was John Wayne who was in town promoting *The Alamo.* He could tell Ida was still getting her feet wet. He took a special liking to her and they stayed in contact through the years.

Paramount Studios invited Ida to meet John Wayne and the crew of *Hatari* in Salt Lake City and travel with them to Denver and on to Dallas. She was with them for four days.

Ida talked to the vice-president of Paramount about using television as a means of critiquing and promoting movies. She was offered a television talk show in Los Angeles called *Dateline Hollywood.* Ida did not want to move her children to California. She talked to John Kirkpatrick, one of the leading investors at Channel Five who allowed her to become a correspondent for *Dateline Hollywood* here in Oklahoma City, and added that segment to her program. Years later, she joked with Mr. Kirkpatrick, saying that he found a way for her to keep her son Bobby in Oklahoma. Now Bob Blackburn is known as the leading historian in the state.

Paramount agreed to her filming the show in Oklahoma City but wanted her to go to Los Angeles for two week's training. However, she would have to pay her own way. She had made many friends on her show and now contacted them. Chevrolet loaned her a new white convertible, Sheraton Hotels gave her a suite for two weeks, and some of the movie exhibiters sent her one hundred dollars each to pay for her airfare. In 1962, *Dateline Hollywood* began and Ida became one of the first television correspondents in the nation.

For Ida, this was a year filled with premiers and Hollywood openings as she traveled to the entertainment capitols of the world to cover premiers and interview stars. This also put her on the "must stop" list for entertainers promoting their movies or traveling across the country. On her show, she interviewed Bob Hope, Jimmy Stewart, Natalie Wood, Kim Novack, Doris Day, Agnes Morehead, Debbie Reynolds, Paul Newman, Joanne Woodward, Tony Curtis, Jack Lemon and many others.

Ida was fortunate that her sister lived nearby, and Bobby and Betty stayed with her and her three children when Ida was out of town. They enjoyed traveling with her when possible but said, "No one knows us by our own names, we're Ida B's kids."

She told them, "some day, I'll be known as Bob's mother and Betty's mom."

In 1963, the *Ida "B" Show* was born. Fans turned on her program every morning, six days a week, to be amused, entertained and informed. She featured news on fashions, hair styling trends, events, weather and general reporting on Oklahoma affairs. The station wanted her to avoid topics of religion and politics but she could host politicians like Governor Bartlett or Lieutenant Governor Nigh and talk on other subjects. She hosted the controversial Clara Luper but never received complaints from viewers.

On the early shows, Ida did her own commercials, either by memory or ad-libbing. On Thursdays she cooked for Safeway, and the recipes were available at the stores. She also advertised for C.R. Anthony. When TG&Y built their family centers, she explored a different department on her show each week. One week the guest was the floral designer, the next time featured a clothing style show, followed by a tour of the furniture department, and another week the automobile repair shop was featured.

Ida did not script her shows. Her philosophy was never to pre-interview anyone, so that her time with a guest would be as fresh to her as to the viewers. Spontaneity was the key to interesting stories that might not have come up otherwise. Variety was another element to her shows. She promoted organizations and fundraisers and featured children's performances.

From 1968 to 1974, Ida promoted local concerts. In 1968, she sponsored an Eddie Arnold Concert and in 1973 she filled the Myriad Convention Center with fans of Charlie Pride. She received a proclamation from Mayor Patience Latting for assembling the largest crowd in the state of Oklahoma for an indoor event. Channel Five was instrumental in providing funding for the opening of the Cowboy Hall of Fame and she helped with many events there.

Ida hosted *The Ida "B* show for fifteen years until in 1975, her time slot was filled by the network show, *Good Morning America*. During those television years she received many public service awards for her work in community affairs. She was appointed Chairman of the General Safety Communications for the Greater Oklahoma City Safety Council. She was chosen for Who's Who in Women in Communications and Women in Variety. She served as co-chairman of Women's Gridiron of Oklahoma, and is a member of American Women in Radio and Television.

After her show ended, Ida became the first woman to sell advertising for the television station. Her start in sales was not easy. She was up against an all male staff at KOCO and an Oklahoma marketplace that was composed largely of male clients. Within five years she was the top sales person.

She resigned from KOCO-TV in 1985 to become a communication consultant and to open her own ad agency. She later joined Trans-Media Communication as a media specialist.

Ida was proud that in 2001, she was inducted into the Oklahoma Journalism Hall of Fame, proving that journalism is not just the written word.

She believes that television is losing its personal contact. News commentators should talk to the viewers instead of their co-anchors. Television should be a living body and a personal experience of mutual respect between the viewer and the person on the screen. Good advice from a lady, who at one time was voted the top local television personality in the country.

Alma Wilson, Chief judge of the Oklahoma Supreme Court. Photo courtesy of the Oklahoma Historical Society.

Alma Bell Wilson

Chief Justice on the Oklahoma Supreme Court

In 1982, one year after Sandra Day O'Connor became the first woman appointed to the United States Supreme Court, Governor George Nigh named Alma Bell Wilson to the Oklahoma Supreme Court. Governor Nigh made it clear that she was not appointed because of her gender but because she was the most qualified. From 1995 to 1997 Alma Wilson served as Chief Justice of the Oklahoma Supreme Court.

Alma Bell Wilson has been called "the people's judge". In some circles she is known as Oklahoma's Judge Judy. Long before the television show, Alma Wilson was dispensing outspoken advice with a wry sense of humor. Rather than grant divorces she told disgruntled spouses to go home and work it out. She locked up trouble-making teenagers in jail overnight on charges she specifically wrote to scare some sense into them. Without the benefit of television cameras or national publicity, Alma Wilson rose to the state's highest court and a place in Oklahoma history.

W.R. Bell, Alma's father, owned an abstract office and served as mayor of Pauls Valley. Alma remembered him as a "Missouri Democrat" who wished that he had been a lawyer. He transferred this desire to his daughter. He wanted one of his twin girls to become a lawyer. He had no idea how high his dreams would rise.

Alma and her sister Wilma were born May 25, 1917, in Pauls Valley. Anna, their mother, was the daughter of German immigrants. She delighted in her girls. An expert seamstress, she made most of their clothes.

The twins usually dressed alike, however their personalities proved they were two distinct people. Alma talked to anyone she could corner. Wilma, on the other hand, was shy and less assertive. For their entire lives, the girls remained close friends.

From age five Alma and Wilma took piano, dancing, and public speaking lessons. They performed for most Pauls Valley community organizations.

Once a week, Will and Anna drove the girls to Oklahoma City, a rough 60-mile trip in a Model T Ford, to tap dance on an early Sunday morning show on WKY radio. The twins also read the parts of the children in the Katzenjammer Kids comic strip on the show.

At the age of eight, Alma announced that she wanted to become an attorney. Women lawyers were a rarity in 1925. Most Americans believed that a woman's place was in the home. When Alma Bell voiced her intention, fewer than forty female lawyers were practicing in the state of Oklahoma.

Alma's childhood friends regarded her as extremely smart. She starred in the school's theatrical productions and played the piano for the glee club. She was valedictorian of Pauls Valley High School Class of 1935, consisting of 23 boys and 22 girls. Alma performed three different functions for the graduation ceremony. She played the piano as students marched in, ran to the stage to deliver her valedictory address, then returned to the piano to accompany the class as they left the auditorium.

There was never any doubt that the Bell girls would attend college, even though most of their female counterparts were content to marry, have children and never seek education beyond high school.

Alma and Wilma began their higher education at Principia College in Elsah, Illinois, a private school for children of Christian Scientist faith. For the first time in their lives the twins were not allowed to room together. Both girls worked part-time to help pay tuition. They played basketball and field hockey, and their freshman basketball team went undefeated. Alma joined the Principia Dramatic Club.

Because of the Depression and their father's failing health, the twins decided Principia was too expensive for them to return for a second year. They enrolled, instead, at Oklahoma City University. When OCU became too expensive, they transferred to the University of Oklahoma. Tuition for each of the sisters was $17.50 a semester. With money saved, they were able to join Chi Omega Sorority, but limited funds kept them from living in the house. Alma became a huge OU football fan, a passion that would consume fall Saturday afternoons for the rest of her life.

During the Christmas break, OU made their first-ever trip to the Orange Bowl and after a long battle with cancer, W.R. Bell died January 4, 1938.

In the spring of 1938, after only three years of college, Alma graduated with a Bachelors degree in English and a minor in French. She enrolled with three other freshman women in the OU School of Law. Only 14 women made up the 312 students in the school. Alma and five other women were among the 1941 OU College of Law graduating class of 100.

Even though she held a job while in school, she was in the top one-third of her class academically,

In the 1940's only 2.4 per cent of the nation's lawyers were women. It was not at all unusual for women to be low in number in graduate schools – only three freshman woman enrolled in the OU College of Medicine in 1938.

Wilma was also pursuing a career in a male dominated field. She began her senior year, in 1938, as one of only two women in the accounting department at OU. After graduation, she went to work as an accountant with the State Examiner and Inspectors office in Oklahoma City.

In April, 1941, Alma passed the bar examination with the highest score ever for a woman at that time. While waiting for her bar examination results, Alma was fortunate to find work as a law clerk with United States District Judge Eugene S. Rice in Muskogee. She believed this association was beneficial for her career.

As Alma entered the work force she found career prospects for women lawyers dim. Only 125 women were members of the Oklahoma Bar Association. When female attorneys applied for a job, they were often asked, "Can you type?"

In 1942, she was hired as a staff lawyer for the Midland Valley Railroad in Muskogee. Many years later she discovered the reason they'd hired her was because, as a female, she could not be drafted for the war effort.

Sister Wilma married Mickey Snufflebean, and they settled in Pauls Valley. Alma's mother, Anna, lived with her in Muskogee and at the birth of Wilma's first child, they realized how homesick they were for central Oklahoma and their family. Alma gave up her job with the railroad and moved her mother back to Oklahoma City. She went to work as an investigator for the Office of Price Administration while she looked for a job in a law firm.

She was hired by the Oklahoma City firm of Campbell, Randolph, Mosteller, and McElroy. Soon her name was added to the door –but was listed as A.D. Bell. The senior partners did not want any possible prejudice from the fact that a woman lawyer was a member of the firm.

In 1946, she moved to Howard K. Berry's law firm as a junior partner. There, she met Bill Wilson, another junior partner, and they were married in 1948. They moved into an apartment in Pauls Valley where Bill was hired as assistant county attorney.

Their only child Lee Anne was born three years later. Alma felt fortunate that for the next few years she had the luxury of staying home with her daughter. When Lee Anne started school, Alma took a more active part in her husband's firm which specialized in personal injury litigation. Constantly busy, she balanced her time as a wife and mother, practicing law, serving as president of the Pauls Valley Parent Teacher Association, the local chapter of the American Association of University Women and the Mother's Study Club. She also learned to fly the couple's Piper Comanche and joined the 99's, an organization of women pilots.

In 1964, shortly before Lee Anne's 13th birthday, Bill suffered a severe stroke. While he recuperated, Alma took over the day-to-day work at the law firm. In 1965, she became Pauls Valley's Municipal Judge.

No stranger to being "first," Alma was appointed a special district judge for Garvin and McClain counties. After a few months on the job, a newspaper reporter wrote, "The diminutive jurist has lent an atmosphere of grace and charm to the dignity of the walnut paneled Garvin County courtroom." In the same article, Alma was quoted as saying, "A woman doing a man's work can not be mediocre in any respect. Women need to excel."

Oklahoma City Judge Terry Pendell said three of the first women judges, Alma Wilson, Arthur Lory Rakestraw, and Terry Pendell met in Moore, once a month for dinner and discussion of the various triumphs and problems of being a female judge.

Judge Pendell was, in 1975, the first woman to be appointed a judge in Oklahoma City, and Judge Rakestraw was appointed by Oklahoma Governor David Boren as a district judge in Oklahoma County.

Terry also said she and Alma served on the Board of Directors of the Association of Women Judges and attended national judges' conventions in Atlanta, Washington, and San Francisco together. She said Alma was well respected across the country as wanting to make things easier for other female judges. She was also known for "letting her hair down and having a good time."

Alma had her own opinion of the women's rights movement. She said, "I don't think women want something for nothing like many other movements. Some of their arguments are valid. However, I think women's liberation, should be accomplished by the individual excelling and making a place for herself. Generally speaking, any women who can do the job will not be discriminated against."

Alma served as special judge for McClain and Garvin counties from 1969 to 1975 when Governor David Boren appointed her the first woman district judge for Cleveland County. That same year she was named Woman of the Year by the Business and Professional Women's Club and was inducted into the University of Oklahoma Alumni Hall of Fame.

Alma managed to keep up her tennis game.

Terry Pendell noted that Alma took out her frustrations on the tennis court, yelling, "This one is for justice" as she whacked the ball.

Alma also enjoyed dinner and dancing at the OU University Club in Norman. There, she and Bill developed a friendship with Paul and Doris Travis. Doris had danced in the *Ziegfeld Follies*, and they shared a common belief in Christian Science.

Alma was known by her colleagues to be fair and tough. When she was appointed to replace the late Ben T. Williams on the Oklahoma Supreme Court, it was more a surprise to her than to other state attorneys.

Governor George Nigh picked Judge Wilson from a list of three nominees submitted to him by the state Judicial Nominating Commission. He said he did not choose her just to appoint the first woman for historic reasons, but because she met all the qualifications.

He commented, "I said to myself, 'Why should I appoint a woman?' And then I said to myself, 'why shouldn't I appoint a woman?' I just tried to be fair."

In the book "*Good Guys Wear White Hats: The Life of George Nigh*," author Bob Burke wrote, "There was much speculation in the press as to whom George would appoint to the state's highest court. When House Judiciary Chairman, Representative Robert Henry of Shawnee, went to George's office to support Wilson's candidacy, George said, "Line up with all the others, Alma Wilson apparently has a lot of friends."

Governor Nigh told Alma, "You have paid your dues, you have an excellent record as a judge, you're liked by most everyone, you deserve to be on the Supreme Court."

Shortly after 11:00 a.m., on February 17, 1982, Chief Justice Pat Irwin administered the oath of office in the packed chambers of the Oklahoma House of Representatives. Alma introduced Bill, Lee Anne, Wilma and Nathan, and others, then she spoke of her father and mother. She said, "It was mother, Annabelle, who could not be here today (she had broken her hip and was confined to a nursing home in Pauls Valley), whose quiet strength and perseverance made this possible. To my father, the late W.R. Bell, I dedicate today, because it was he who inspired my decision, at a very young age, to study law."

Alma told one newspaper correspondent, "I never thought I would sit on the state Supreme Court, and I never thought I would be the first female justice. I don't think of it as being a woman judge - I think of it as being a judge."

Having a woman on the Supreme Court presented the problem of what to call a female justice: Madam Justice, Your Honor, or Mrs. Justice Wilson. The unpretentious judge said, "Why don't you call me Alma?"

In the book *Justice Served: The Life of Alma Wilson*, Bob Burke and Louise Painter, told the story of Justice John Doolin, Alma's former college classmate. This fellow Justice of the Supreme Court had his own name for Alma and the court –"Alma and the Supremes."

Alma took the joking in stride saying, "If I don't make good on the Supreme Court, I might make it in a singing group."

The month following her swearing in, Alma was a guest speaker at a University of Central Oklahoma seminar in honor of National Women's History Week. Joining her were old friends and colleagues, Oklahoma City Municipal Judge Terry Pendell and District Judge Lory Rakestraw, both well respected female members of the Oklahoma bar.

Alma told the audience, "Life is one big endurance contest and women have better endurance."

Judge Pendell, who later served as a judge on the Oklahoma Workers' Compensation Court, encouraged other women to share in sisterhood in the professional areas. She said, "We need a network of 'good old girls' so we can help one another."

After serving for a year, Judge Wilson's name went on the judicial retention ballot. She easily received the vote to be retained for the remaining portion of Justice Williams' term. She, then was retained by the voters in 1984, 1986, and 1992. She served as Chief Justice for a two year term in 1995-96, the first woman Justice and Chief Justice of the Oklahoma Supreme Court.

Although she was considered stern on the bench, Judge Wilson loved to have a good time. Serious and calm when hearing cases, she was known to yell with the best of them when cheering her beloved Sooners.

Doris Travis tells that both she and Alma were inducted into the Oklahoma Hall of Fame at the same time. That night, Alma joined her on the stage in a soft-shoe routine.

Alma personified women who entered a male-dominated field, and through diligent work, garnered the respect of her peers. Her achievements have been recognized through many awards, including induction into the Oklahoma Women's Hall of Fame, by the Governor's committee on the Status of Woman. She received the University of Oklahoma's Outstanding Achievement Award and the Pioneer Woman Award. She was named Appellate Judge of the Year in 1986 and in 1989, and named to the Oklahoma Hall of Fame in 1996.

Alma was nominated to the Oklahoma Hall

of Fame by Louise Painter, who noted, "In true pioneer spirit she has cut a pathway for other women to follow."

Her nomination was seconded by a prestigious group, including United States Supreme Court Justice Sandra Day O'Connor who said, "She is a physically small bundle of enormous dedication and action, with a lifetime of achievement in the legal profession." University of Oklahoma President David Boren, said, "She opened new doors for women." Mrs. Fred Jones said, "I know of no one who deserves the honor more." Oklahoma Bar Association President, Mona Lambird, called Alma "one of a kind."

Many more letters were written, but they can be summed up by the nomination from United States District Judge Lee R. West who said, "She was a pioneer and pursued her profession with a determined grace that firmly established her a force to be reckoned with, regardless of gender."

Although she kept on working, Alma became ill in 1999. A private person, she did not want people to know that she had been diagnosed with leukemia. She died at her Oklahoma City home on July 27, 1999, at age 82.

Lt. Governor Mary Fallin ordered state flags to be flown at half mast. A public memorial service was held at the Paul Sharp Concert Hall at the University of Oklahoma.

Alma's friend and comrade on the Supreme Court, Justice Yvonne Kauger, said, "I am certain that the halls of heaven ring with the click of her high heels as she attacks her next project."

University of Oklahoma President, David Boren, who had appointed Alma as district judge a quarter century before said, "Through her integrity and devotion to the rule of law, Justice Wilson left a lasting mark on our state."

Donna Nigh

"Good Girls Wear White Hats"

Through their distinguished political and volunteer careers, Donna and George Nigh were a team and known as "good guys." While supportive of the Governor's activities Donna carved her own identity through her many accomplishments. A powerful advocate for mental retardation programs, Donna has been the guiding force in improving the quality of life for Oklahomans with developmental disabilities. She innovated in, 1981, the establishment of group homes in Oklahoma. Now, with more than 100 facilities statewide, the Donna Nigh Group Home Program provides an opportunity for the disabled to live and function in a community. In 1998, President Clinton appointed her to the President's Committee on Mental Retardation. Group homes initiated by Donna Nigh are models for other homes across the nation.

As a child, Donna never imagined she would one day be Oklahoma's first lady. She was born in Morris, to Raphael and Gertha Mae Dunham Skinner, and grew up in South Oklahoma City where her parents owned a neighborhood grocery store. Later her father managed the Skinner's coffee shop in the Oklahoma Natural Gas Building downtown. Donna spent her high school summers waiting tables there.

A strong supporter of South Oklahoma City, Donna is proud that she graduated from Capitol Hill

High School. Active in pep club and other organizations, she has great memories of those early days.

A group of Donna's friends from Capitol Hill High School still enjoy getting together. The Naughty Nine, as they called themselves, for many years traveled each summer and had dinner together during the Christmas season. Recently, they lost three of their members and have forgone the trips but still reunite at least once a year.

Following high school, Donna attended Central State College, now the University of Central Oklahoma in Edmond. A reservation agent for Trans World Airlines at the Skirvin Hotel in Oklahoma City, she was talked into a blind date with handsome former Governor George Nigh. Thirty six year old George had served as Lieutenant Governor and as Governor for nine days when Governor J. Howard Edmonson resigned to fill Robert S. Kerr's position as United States Senator.

Herman Harmon, a reservation agent for American Airlines arranged a get-acquainted Coke date for Donna and George at the Skirvin Tower Coffee Shop. George said it was love at first sight. Donna wasn't so sure. The newspapers referred to George as the state's most eligible bachelor, but Donna says, "I didn't know what the big deal was. He didn't have a car, a home or a job. I had all three."

Donna was not accustomed to appearing in public with a face that everyone knew. From a previous marriage, she had an eleven-year-old son, Berry Michael "Mike" Mashburn. Although he liked George, Mike didn't want to share his mother.

Donna had done well as a single mother and was reluctant to change her status, but within six months, she accepted George's proposal. The couple was married October 19, 1963, and one of the states most noted partnerships began.

By that time, George headed a public relations firm, promoting and managing conventions in his home state. He had also gained a national reputation as a motivational speaker. However, he began thinking of re-entering public office. Donna pledged support in whatever he decided to do.

The family's joy was made complete on January 14, 1965, when Donna gave birth to a seven-pound, thirteen ounce daughter, Georgeann. Twelve-year-old Mike was a proud big brother.

George was again elected Lieutenant Governor, November 8, 1966, serving with Republican Governor Dewey Bartlett. Donna traveled with George on inspections of state facilities, from hospitals and other institutions to colleges and universities. It was during these visits of the three state schools for the mentally retarded that she became interested in their plight. She felt like they were a forgotten part of our population, and that many did not belong in institutions.

Donna volunteered her services at the Dale Rogers Center and the Association for Retarded Citizens. At a conference for Lieutenant Governors, she learned of group homes in another state. She began investigating problems of the mentally handicapped.

Part of a lieutenant governor's job was to appear at hundreds of local celebrations held each year. George and Donna attended as many as possible, as well as promoting tourism at many out of state events.

In 1978, George decided to run for the office of Governor. Donna, again was a faithful campaigner, reportedly packing in larger crowds than George. His chief opponents for the Democratic primary were Attorney General Larry Derryberry and State Senator Bob Funston, both personal friends.

Derryberry labeled George as a "good guy" too good to be governor. Derryberry said, "If you want a good guy, vote for Nigh. If you want a good governor, vote for me."

George's response was, "What's wrong with being a good guy? For 28 years I've been trying to build the voters' confidence by conducting myself in a manner of which they would be proud." The good guy image became the Nigh campaign theme.

The question arose, "What do good guys wear?" Thus came the now famous white hats, tee-shirts, boots, and "good guy" stickers.

Donna and George loved campaigning. Sometimes they traveled together, sometimes in separate caravans, by both car and airplane. Campaign funds were far less than any of the other candidates, but they depended on grass root support from individuals and communities. They visited at least one town in each of Oklahoma's 77 counties.

Martin Hauan, political commentator, was quoted in Bob Burke's book *Good Guys Wear White Hats:* "Donna often got more notice than George. George has been some places so often, he is old hat. Not Donna. She has a lively personality and can and will speak on the issue. She was also blessed with the livest-wire sidekick around, Shirley Cassil... Like Donna, you can see in her face what she thinks. I promise you this pair made votes wherever they went."

George remembered Donna's impact on the campaign. "She's an issue person more than a tea-sipper. We had people on the caravans who would rather go with her than me. We had press asking to go with her. She's strong, knowledgeable, discussing issues from my vantage point but not afraid to come right out with how she feels."

Donna said she misses the old style campaigning. "Nowadays, it is who can raise the most money and buy television advertising. The candidates and the people miss out on the personal connection."

Donna Nigh, First Lady of Oklahoma.   Photo, Courtesy of Donna Nigh.

George was elected governor and Donna chose her high school friend and campaign buddy Shirley Cassil to be her secretary. Donna said Shirley didn't know how to be a secretary, but that was OK as *she* didn't know how to be First Lady. They got along beautifully- and still do. The important thing was Shirley knew how to deal with people, and she was a second mother to Georgeann.

Donna began redecorating the Governor's mansion. Former governors had been required to provide their own bedroom and living room furniture, so the sprawling house was basically empty when George and Donna surveyed what would be their home for the next eight years. In 1979, when the Nighs took up residence, none of the original furniture remained except for a hall tree on the second floor landing.

The mansion needed rewiring, new carpet, energy efficient windows, and sandblasting of the Indiana limestone exterior. There was almost always water in the basement from a continuous leak.

Donna liked to point out that the mansion and George were born the same year, and that she "had to have the mansion sandblasted." She also gave George a 1927 radio and says she had it rewired, just like the old house.

There was no decorating budget. Donna used antique chairs and tables she discovered in storage rooms in the capitol, and furniture she brought from their old home. In rummaging through the mansion and the capitol basement, she found treasures, including doors for the bookcases in the living room. She rescued and researched many of these forgotten items from past administrations.

Then she invited all Oklahoma to come visit, saying, "The mansion belongs to the people. We want to make sure it's accessible to the public."

Against advice, she opened the house to public tours on Wednesday afternoons. Not only the first floor, but the second floor living quarters were viewed. By 1982, 20,000 people annually toured the mansion.

At first Donna greeted every guest. People stopped and talked with her, holding up the lines of visitors. Eventually, she began running errands away from home during open house.

Tour guides frequently were asked, "Which side of the bed does the Governor sleep on?" Donna said often visitors left messages under her pillow, asking her to intercede with the governor for a favor.

Donna was proud of her remodeling efforts on little money. She said, that later Cathy Keating, and her founding of the Friends of the Mansion, really made the house a beautiful place that all Oklahoman's can be proud of. Donna serves as an honorary member of that committee.

She found that her days of running around the house barefoot and in her nightgown, were over. She had always cleaned her own house and cooked her own meals. Believing she didn't need to waste the taxpayers' money on a cook, she soon found that sometimes 20 guests were served breakfast. There might be 40 for lunch, and 80 people at the mansion for dinner. She changed her mind about a cook. It was hard to adapt to security that accompanied her everywhere, even while shopping or going to church. But she laughed and commented that at least she had gotten four State Troopers back in church.

Donna felt that former first ladies were ignored after their tenures, and she invited them to a luncheon along with mansion volunteers.

As first lady, she met with Department of Public Safety officials to remove practices in the state's driver education and testing program that discriminated against the handicapped. She served on the Mother's March of Birth Defects and chaired Oklahoma's Cancer Fund Drive. She was responsible for legislation for mandatory immunization for all school age children and requiring approved car seats for youngsters.

Her favorite project was an annual Easter egg hunt given for blind children on the mansion grounds. She hosted students from the School for the Blind in Muskogee and other public and private schools and institutions serving non-sighted children. Costumed characters such as Mr. and Mrs. Easter Bunny assisted with the hunt. The Oklahoma Grocers Association gave each child huge baskets filled with candy, cookies, and toys.

The Pioneers, a group of retired employees of Western Electric, installed beepers in plastic eggs. All the children, including those with partial sight, were blindfolded to make the egg hunt fair. Children scrambled around the mansion grounds in search of beeping eggs. One television station broadcast a child holding a live rabbit, asking the reporter, "Is he pretty?"

Donna never forgot her visits to the state schools and her vow to someday help these people. "I felt like a lot of them could function in an outside world. I wanted to establish a group home system for them. Some states were doing very well with this concept.

When George decided to run for Governor, Donna said she would help him if he would support her efforts to improve the lives of retarded citizens. He replied that he would help, but, she would have to do her own lobbying.

Donna investigated Oklahoma's property

laws, and community interest, as well as problems with group homes elsewhere. She visited with the Department of Human Services, the Health Department and the Department of Mental Health. She studied fire marshal codes and zoning laws. She discovered that the state could not own property so she found groups willing to sponsor the projects. By the time she approached the legislature, she was ready for their questions. She learned that lobbying was not easy, and how difficult it was to start a new program.

Finally in 1981, the legislature approved funding for a pilot program to establish 10 group homes. Funding now is budgeted through the Department of Human Services, Developmental Disabilities Services Division, and has been identified officially in state government as the Donna Nigh Group Home Program.

Numbering more that 100 statewide, the homes provide opportunities for the mentally retarded to live and function in a community. Residents must hold down a job or work in a sheltered workshop and be virtually medication free. In the beginning, some communities were leery of group homes but have found the residents to be good neighbors.

As a gift for her birthday in 1984, a group of Donna's friends created the Donna Nigh Foundation, the only statewide organization for the developmentally disabled. The foundation continues to award small grants to group homes and sheltered workshops as well as to individuals who do not qualify for government aid. They often provide playground equipment, assist in making a van handicapped accessible, or purchase special computers. The foundation presented $50,000 to the Oklahoma City Public School Foundation to bring buildings up

to code, making facilities accessible to the handicapped.

In the past Donna has organized many
fundraisers for this cause —a garage sale at the
mansion, statewide chili suppers, and Academy
Award parties. Now, the fund is managed by the
Oklahoma City Community Foundation although
Donna is still the chairman and has the final say on
grants.

In 1998, President Clinton asked Donna to
serve as a member of the President's Committee on
Retardation, which she did for five years. She served
with 17 members from across the United States, who
met in Washington four or five times a year.

After George's second term as Governor, he
served as president of the University of Central Oklahoma from1992 to1997. There, he started the Nigh
Institute for Government Studies and Donna established a university art gallery that has since been
named for her. University life was a new experience
for Donna. She enjoyed relating to the younger generation.

In 1999, the legislature and Governor Frank
Keating approved funding for the George and Donna
Nigh Public Service Scholarship. Each year, $100,000
is awarded for scholarships for students to attend a
conference on public service. Each college is given
$1,000 for a student to attend the three-day confer-
ence. This award is very meaningful to the Nighs. In
announcing the scholarship, Higher Education
Chancellor Hans Brisch said, "We can only hope that
the recipients of the George and Donna Nigh Public
Service awards will follow in their footsteps and give
back to Oklahoma in meaningful ways."

In 1993, Donna was inducted into the Oklahoma Women's Hall of Fame. She was named the
1997 Wall of Fame honoree by the Oklahoma City

Public School Foundation. She has received the Women in Communication Byline Award in Health, the Pioneer Women Award, and named the Distinguished Former Student at the University of Central Oklahoma. In 2003, she was listed as one of the "100 Notable Women of Style" by *Oklahoma Today* magazine.

In April of 2006, The Oklahoma Health Center Foundation honored George and Donna as 2006 Living Treasure Award recipients. With four others, they were honored as "models for quality values and goodness because of their passions for life, courage and inspiring actions."

In addition to the Donna Nigh Foundation, Donna presently serves on the boards of the City Rescue Mission, Oklahoma Foundation for Excellence, and Friends of the Mansion. She is a deacon at Westminster Presbyterian Church where she in charge of the flowers and tutors at-risk children from Horace Mann School.

Twice a month, she plays mah-jongg, is taking organ lessons, and spends as much time as possible with her seven grandchildren. She and George enjoy visiting with the large circle of friends they have made through the years.

Donna Nigh served sixteen years as the wife of the Lieutenant Governor and eight as the wife of the Governor. She is grateful for that time and says her volunteer activities are a way of paying Oklahoma back for a good life. A favorite quotation is by Muhammad Ali, "Service to others is the rent you pay for your room here on earth."

"That quote keeps me focused. I want to give back because I have been so fortunate."

Reba McEntire, First Lady of Country Music. Photo, Courtesy of Starstruck entertainment.

Reba McEntire

Leading Lady of Country Music

Reba McEntire has been singing songs and collecting awards for over twenty years, winning among others fifteen American Music Awards, 12 Academy of Country Music Awards, and two Grammy's. She has sold more than 50 million albums in her career. She has also performed in ten movies and won rave reviews for her starring role on Broadway in "Annie Get Your Gun." Her TV show "REBA" just wrapped up it's fifth season, and has landed Reba a Golden Globe nomination and a People's Choice Award. She has premiered her own clothing line. Reba is also well known for her service to others and has received the Humanitarian award from the County and Music Association. Her career now reaches far beyond country music, but she's never forgotten her Oklahoma upbringing.

Walking through the Will Rogers International Airport, you are apt to hear over the loud speaker, "Hi, I'm Reba McEntire. Welcome to my home state of Oklahoma, where we will be celebrating one hundred years of statehood in 2007. Happy Birthday Oklahoma!"

That voice is known all over the world as the most successful country artist in history, with two Grammy Awards, a string of multi- platinum LP's and number one singles, a successful television show and many acting credits, but Reba's roots are in Oklahoma.

Reba Nell McEntire, named after her grand-mother Reba Estelle Brassfield, was born March 28, 1955, in McAlester, Oklahoma, She was the daughter of rodeo champion Clark Vincent McEntire and schoolteacher Jacqueline Smith McEntire. She grew up on the family ranch at Chockie with her brother Pake and two sisters Alice and Susie. Pake's real name is Del Stanley but no one would know him by that name. He received his nickname even before he was born.

Rodeo's and ranching were the way of life for the McEntire family. Her dad owned 8,000 acres of land and 3,000 head of cattle. The children were the ranch hands. They rode horses from the time they were old enough to sit in the saddle. Reba remembers a rodeo announcer saying "If you want to keep your kid's out of trouble, put them on a horse."

By the time Reba was six she was gathering cattle before daylight and often until late evening. In addition to outside chores, she and her sisters helped their mother with the cooking and house-work. Ranch life was not easy. Still, Reba has great memories of those days, especially the trouble the kids managed to get into, like the time their parents were gone and Pake dared Alice to ride a steer. She ran into the cattle pen and cut her head open. Or the time Susie's horse got away from her and ran into the house and then into a clothesline. As soon as their daddy would release them from their chores, the kid's would head for the roping pens. They would ride barrels, rope, or turn out the cattle for Pake to rope until dark.

Her father was a three-time world champion steer roper, winning in 1957, '58, and '61. His father, John McEntire won the steer roping champi-onship in 1934.

Needless to say family entertainment was

traveling the rodeo circuit. They didn't have a car radio so when the children, in the back seat, would get rowdy or bored their mother taught the youngsters to sing three-part harmony.

Reba has always given her parents credit for her success - her mother gave her the love of music and singing talent, and her daddy taught her a strong work ethic and discipline.

As soon as they were old enough each child began competing in rodeos. Pake, also, became a champion steer roper. Reba began competing when she was eleven years old and ran barrels until she was 21.

She sang for the first time professionally, when she was four years old, on a rodeo trip to Cheyenne, Wyoming. In a large crowd, at the Edwards hotel lobby, someone paid her brother Pake, 25 cents to sing "Hound Dog." Not wanting to be left out Reba sang "Jesus Loves Me" for a nickel. That was the first time she realized you could get paid for singing.

In the first grade, she sang "Away in a Manger" during a Christmas program in the high school gymnasium. She liked singing into a microphone.

Kiowa High School did not have enough students for a marching band, so Reba, Pake, and Susie formed the school's first and only Kiowa Cowboy High School Band. Reba, Pake and Susie also formed a singing group known as *The Singing McEntire's* who sang for school events and honky-tonks and dance halls. They had a bit of success with a single, "The Ballad of John McEntire," dedicated to their grandfather.

Reba enjoyed singing but at that time her first love was barrel racing. After she graduated high school, she competed in about fifty rodeos a year.

After high school, she attended Southeastern Oklahoma State University in Durant, majoring in elementary education with a minor in music. She became a member of Chorvettes, a singing and dancing group that performed on campus and in neighboring towns. Reba said she thinks she would have made a good teacher, but fans across the world are happy that her life took a different turn.

Rodeo people have always felt a certain ownership of Reba as she sang at rodeo's before she hit the "big time." In 1974, she was 19, when Clem McSpadden invited her to sing the National Anthem at the National Finals Rodeo in Oklahoma City. Country music legend Red Stegall was in the audience. He persuaded her to go to Nashville and pitch her talents to some of the record companies. November 11, 1975, Reba signed with Mercury Records. The first song she recorded was "Invitation to the Blues."

In 1976, Reba received her teaching degree and married Rodeo Cowboy Association's three-time champion steer wrestler Charlie Battles. They were married June 21st at the Stringtown Baptist Church. The couple bought a ranch near there, in Southeastern Oklahoma.

In 1977, Reba released her debut LP *Reba McEntire*. The following year she had her first hit country song with Three Sheets in the Wind. She also appeared for the first time at the Grand Ole Opry. Her family traveled 1400 miles round trip to see her three minute performance. Her act was cut short by a surprise visit from Dolly Parton. Reba remembered the first time she went to the Grand Ole Opry when she was seven years old. Feeling sick, she ran outside during the show and threw up on the front steps. Reba joined the cast of the Opry in 1986.

Throughout the 80's and 90's Reba became the most successful country artist in history with a string of multi-platinum LPs, number one singles and awards.

Reba toured with her own group the Chockie Mountain Band and also toured with other well-known artist such as The Statler Brothers, Ricky Skaggs, Charlie Pride, Mel Tillis, and T.C Sheppard. Reba's first touring bus, "Old May" was bought in 1982. Before that she had been traveling in trucks, vans, and cars with horse trailers full of equipment.

By 1996, her concert tour featured 16 trucks, 7 buses, 1 jet, 100 tour date 200-foot expandable stage, 3 separate performance areas, 10 dancers, video cameras, 6 video screens, 96 person crew and 40 tons of equipment.

Reba hit the country Top 10 for the first time with "You Lift Me Up to Heaven" in 1980. In 1984, she won the Country Music Association Award for Female Vocalist of the Year and won an Academy of Country Music award for Top Female Vocalist of the Year. The next two years she captured both of these awards, plus in 1986, she received the coveted award for Entertainer of the Year and the video of the year by the Country Music Association. By winning the CMA female vocalist of the year more than once, Reb joined a select group that includes Dolly Parton, Loretta Lynn, and Barbara Mandrell.

Oklahoma honored their favorite daughter on November 15, 1987 at the Oklahoma Hall of Fame Induction ceremony by naming Reba, Ambassador of Goodwill. She also won a Grammy Award for Best Country Vocal performance.

Reba divorced her husband of eleven years in 1987. She relinquished their 214 acre Oklahoma ranch and moved to Nashville. She also won her fourth country music Association award for Female vocalist of the year and an Academy of Country Award for Top Female Vocalist.

Reba debuted at Carnegie Hall on October 26, 1987. The show was a sellout.

In 1989, Reba married Narvel Bladkstock. He had started with her in 1980 as her steel guitar player and progressed through the ranks to become her band leader, road manager, tour manager and finally manager and husband. He is still her manager and her best friend.

The multi-talented star made her acting debut in the horror-comedy film *Tremors* in 1990. She also appeared in the films *North* and *The Little Rascals*. On television she starred with Kenny Rogers in the movie *The Gambler Returns: The Luck of the Draw*. She, played the leading female role in the TV movies, *The Man from Left Field.*, and *Buffalo Girls*. By 2006, she has made ten films. Although she enjoys her movie career, she said that she is a very orderly person and it bothers her that movies are not filmed in chronological order. She would like to someday film a good storied western and more comedy roles. She really enjoys comedy and says she comes by it naturally as she was the family and school cutup.

She considers her most fulfilling role to be playing Annie in the Broadway musical *Annie Get Your Gun*. She said she felt that role was her. She grew up wanting to be either Annie Oakley or a champion barrel racer. She received great reviews for that role.

In 1995 The Journal of Country Music said of Reba, "She started out 2 decades ago a honky-tonk inspired farm girl and has ended up a polished, urbane, pop-country proponent..."

Her 1997 tour with Brooks and Dunn was the largest grossing tour in country music history.

She was thrilled when, in 1988, her star was placed on the Hollywood Walk of Fame.

Reba started a new venture in 2001 with the

premier of her new television sitcom, *REBA* on the WB. The show has been very successful and in 2006 has been picked up for a new season with reruns running on Lifetime. In 2004, she was nominated for a Golden Globe Award for best actress in a Musical of Comedy Series. The episodes from the first three years are now available on DVD.

Fans asked, "Is there anything she can't do?" when in 2005 Reba came out with a clothing line. In her grand opening at Dillards Department store in Oklahoma City, even Reba was surprised at the large crowd that attended. She insisted the fashion show not begin until everyone in the audience had a seat. The secret ingredient for the success is Reba's personal approval of each item. Comfort is important. "I thought it would be cool to get my own line that would help women feel more confident. If you feel comfortable, sexy, and strong then the real you is going to come out. If I feel good in what I'm wearing, I have more confidence, whether I am going on stage or out with my family. That's what I wanted to give to other women."

In her spare time she wrote two books, *Reba* with Tom Carter and *Comfort from a Country Quilt.* She managed to write on her laptop computer backstage before and after concerts and while traveling from city to city.

But even success and happiness cannot keep tragedy and heartbreak from occurring. Reba's worst moment came in 1991, when seven of her nine band members were killed in a plane crash. Not only co-workers, they were also good friends. Through it all, Reba learned an important lesson: Life is too short to beat yourself up about the small stuff. She learned to treasure each moment and love your family and friends.

Reba received the Top Humanitarian Award

in 2002 from the Country Music Association. She believes strongly in giving back to the community and to the world what has been given to her. In 1997,she released a song, "What If" and donated all the profits to the Salvation Army.

Many years ago, she became involved with the Texahoma Medical Center in Dennison, Texas, where many people in Southeastern Oklahoma go for treatment. Dr. Darius Maggi asked her to do a benefit and she performed a benefit show for the next fifteen years. She built Reba's Ranch where families of patients could stay for a nominal rate. She also funded a mobile mammography unit that travels in rural Texas and southeastern Oklahoma taking mammograms for people who could not go to the hospital.

She and Narvel also funded the building of two women's buildings in Nashville for Habitat for Humanity. She cut the ribbons for those homes. She became very supportive of this organization and when Whirlpool approached her about appearing on television ads, she readily agreed. She has also given concerts where the proceeds go to Habitat for Humanity.

Reba is excited about the changing face of country music. She sees it becoming popular with the younger generation and with the general population.

In 2006 when the Queen of Country Music was asked in an interview, what award has been the most rewarding, Reba answered " Anything I did that pleased Mama and Daddy."

She said the challenge or struggle to achieve has always been the most exciting. "Then when you get there, you start all over again, " she said.

Reba once asked her daddy if he felt that way about his championship belt buckles for steer roping and he agreed the challenge was the most fun.

One of the most rewarding and touching awards she received was the Mother of the Year Award. She received that in 2005 at the 27th National Mother's Day committee of the Father's Day/ Mother's Day Council. Others receiving the award were talk show host Joy Philbin, celebrity chef Lidia Mattiechio Bastianich, Senior vice- president of Estee Lauder Cosmetics Aerin Lauder, Editor in chief of Allure Magazine Linda Wells, and Chief Excecutive officer of Natori Co, Josie Natori.

In accepting the award Reba said she never expected to receive the award, but noted, "I was raised on a ranch in Oklahoma. The work ethic my momma and daddy taught me is priceless. They taught me that when you say something you mean it for real. It's your word."

Being a mother is the biggest blessing Reba has received. In 2005, when she received the award Reba and Narvel's son, Shelby was fifteen years old. Reba said he is a great kid and she has never had the typical teenage problems with him. When asked how old he was when he realized his mother did not have the typical job. She said, he never questioned it because his best friend was Nathan Dudney, Barbara Mandell's son. They were both driven to school and picked up by their mothers, and their mothers went to work at night. She thinks Shelby will go into the management part of her business.

Narvel's oldest son also helps with the management of Starstruck Entertainement. Reba will be a grandmother, through Narvel's children, for the fifth time in December 2006. That is a role she dearly loves.

She appeared genuinely surprised to be asked what she does to relax. She likes visiting with her family. Pake's middle daughter Calamity lives close and they often just hang out- shop, go to dinner, or to the movies. She enjoys family pictures and making scrapbooks. She said it liked to kill her to make five family scrapbooks last Christmas and she still has five more to go. She likes to read and just finished the sixth book in the Outlander Series.

Reba's feelings about Oklahoma are strong. She said Oklahoma taught her to be honest, hardworking, and gave her a sense of values. She is willing and ready to do anything to support the state she loves.

People have asked Reba why she doesn't change her accent. She said she is proud of that Okie accent and her Oklahoma heritage.

Mary Fallin

Oklahoma's Woman in Politics

A trailblazer in Oklahoma politics, Mary Fallin, in 1994, was the state's first woman, and first Republican, Lieutenant Governor. She was reelected in 1998 and again in 2002. In November of 2006, she became the second woman from Oklahoma to be elected to the United States Congress.

Raised in a family where public service was a family tradition, political life came easy for Mary Fallin. Her father, Joseph "Newton" Copeland served as mayor of Tecumseh until his early death. Her mother, Mary Jo Duggan Copeland, completed his term as mayor and then was elected the town's first woman mayor. Mary's family was involved in most community activities and taught her that public service was a high calling and an important duty.

Although born in Warrensburg, Missouri, December 9, 1954, Mary grew up in Tecumseh, a small town in central Oklahoma, as did her parents and grandparents. She earned a B.S. degree from Oklahoma State University in 1977. After graduation, she moved to Oklahoma City to begin her professional career.

Prior to running for public office, Mary served as the Oklahoma district manager for a national hotel chain. She was named the manager of the year for the company. A working mom, she became involved in leadership roles and volunteer work in the community.

In an article by Phyllis Davis in the August 2000 issue of *Oklahoma Women,* Mary said, "I originally got serious about running for office back in 1989 during the Education Budget HB1017 debate. As I listened more and more to the issues of education, workers' compensation, taxes, gangs, crime, and other family-related issues, I became more and more interested in them as they affected my own child. That fall (1988) the gentleman who had the legislative seat that I ran for decided to resign, and the minute he resigned, I knew that I was supposed to run for office."

She had announced her candidacy for the House of Representatives in December 1989 while still working fulltime and campaigning nights and weekends.

During a campaign stop at a charity event, Mary met a lobbyist at the state capitol, who asked her a series of questions including whether she was pro-life or pro-choice. When she answered that she was pro-life, the man challenged her by asking her what she would do as a young woman running for office if she became pregnant. He insisted she would have to get an abortion because no one would vote for a pregnant woman and that would render her ineffective. Mary was shocked. She told the young man, if she became pregnant, she would run for office and have the baby too. Little did she know that she actually was, at that moment, expecting her second child. Excited about the baby, she faced a tough decision as to whether she should drop out of the race.

Instead, she continued her campaign efforts and in August won the primary election. Thirty days later, she gave birth to a nine-pound boy. Only five weeks remained until the general election. When her son was one week old, Mary was out knocking on doors soliciting votes. Mary was elected in 1990. Her son was five weeks old and her daughter was three.

Mary Fallin, Leiutenant Governor of Oklahoma. Photo, Courtesy of Lieutenant Governor's office.

At age 35, she was elected to the Oklahoma State House of Representatives, District 85. She served in that office from 1990 until she was elected Lieutenant Governor in 1994.

During her tenure as a legislator, Mary was responsible for the passing of seventeen pieces of legislation. She authored legislation that became law in areas ranging from small business health insurance to victims' rights. These included the "stalker law" as well as bills related to health care reform and child support.

In spite of some people's fears that she would be ineffective because of having two small children she was named 1993 Legislator of the Year by the American Legislative Exchange Council and a Small Business Advocate by the National Federation of Independent Business.

Early in Mary's term, first lady Hillary Clinton began a movement to move our nation's healthcare system from a free market approach to one big government run health care system. Mary had taken the role of the leading Republican in the Oklahoma House on health care reform. She was asked by a national conservative group to hold town hall meetings across the state to discuss this issue.

After one of these meetings she was approached about running for Lieutenant Governor. In Oklahoma, no woman had ever won that race, and a Republican had never served in that office. It was also a big risk for Mary who dearly loved the legislature.

Upon her election, Mary was determined not to be merely a ribbon-cutter. She pursued an aggressive agenda focusing on economic development, education, health care and government reform.

As the state's second in command she served

as the President of the Senate. In a historic move in 2000, she took control of the Senate, which caused a three day stand-off between Republicans and Democrats, to bring the issue of Right to Work to a vote of the people for the first time in 25 years. She took control again in 2005 to push for a crucial vote on Workers Compensation Reform.

Mary served on ten boards and commissions that impacted quality of life and business in Oklahoma, including the Tourism and Recreation Commission. State Board of Equalization, Oklahoma Land Commission, State Insurance Fund, and the Film Office Advisory Commission.

During her first term, she served as Chairman of the National Lieutenant Governor's Association. She presided over the association's state/federal meeting in Washington, D.C. and hosted the group's 1998 summer meeting in Oklahoma City. She also has served as the National Chair of the Aerospace States Association and the Republican Lieutenant Governors Association.

She developed a reputation as a pro-business leader, when in 1997 she took aim at Oklahoma's skyrocketing workers compensation cost. The "Fallin Commission" on Workers Compensation Reform" recommended sweeping legal changes to the workers' compensation system, which were later adopted by the Oklahoma legislature.

In 1998, Governor Keating appointed her Oklahoma's Small Business Advocate. In that cabinet-level role, Mary assisted this vital segment of the state's economy with both legislative and individual business concerns. She formed a commission of 300 business owners and representatives to study legislative solutions to the obstacles facing small business. She sponsored Oklahoma's Small

Business Day at the Capitol each year before she left office.

Mary took a special interest in advancing the issues of women business owners and loaned her support and time to events and projects associated with the National Association of Women Business Owners and other organizations that strive to improve the status of women in the workplace.

The protection and future of Oklahoma's children was at the heart of many of the programs she initiated. In the aftermath of the Oklahoma City bombing, Mary formed a task force to rebuild the lost childcare center and raised most of the money. That effort culminated in the summer of 1998 when the YMCA Heartland Child Care Center opened its doors.

Her concern over gun violence and gun safety prompted her to initiate Project Homesafe, a program that has distributed more than 80,000 free cable gun locks to Oklahomans. The program was so successful, she convinced the National Lieutenant Governors Association to adopt the program and took project Homesafe nationwide.

In an effort to help Oklahoma parents better protect their children, she launched a child safety initiative in September, 2002. This included distributing a total of 8,000 free child identification kits at the Oklahoma State Fair, the Tulsa State Fair, Wal-Mart stores and public libraries. Posters promoted tips on how to prevent child abductions.

Her commitment to education was behind the creation of the "Reach for the Stars" banquet to benefit the Community Literacy Center. The center raises funds for the literacy projects across the state. She has served as host of the annual "Reach for the Stars" gala.

As Lieutenant Governor, Mary initiated economic development events including the first ever Oklahoma Aerospace Summit and Expo and Small Business Day at the Capitol. She also hosted the Lt. Governor's invitational Turkey Hunt in five communities across the state, which brought in an average of 70 business prospects each year to hunt turkeys and see Oklahoma.

In June of 2002, she joined the federal Drug Enforcement Administration and other women leaders in government to kick off a national Club Drug Awareness Campaign aimed at fighting club drug use and educating parents and teenagers about the growing use and danger of club drugs such as Ecstasy.

Mary has been a member of the Board of Directors of the United Way of Oklahoma City and the YWCA. She also has served on the Trail of Tears Advisory Board, as Honorary Chair of the Organ Donor Network, Honorary Co-chair of the Indian Territory Arts and Humanities Council, and as co-chair of the "Festival of Hope" organized to promote mental health and wellness. She was a member of Junior Hospitality and Junior League as well of the President of the State Dental Wives.

For her service she has been honored with many awards including Women in Communication's Women in the News Award, Induction into the Oklahoma Women's Hall of Fame, the National Federation of Independent Business' small Business Advocate Award, the Clarence E. Paige Award/Oklahoma Aviation Hall of Fame, Education Advocate of the Year and was named the 1998 Woman of the Year in Government by the Redlands Council of the Girl Scouts. She is a two-time honoree of the *Journal Record's* "50 Making a Difference."

She considers her most important title that

of "mom". She always put her daughter Christina and son Price's activities on her schedule first and you would see Mary at her children's sporting and school events. She likes reading, visits to the lake, and working in her yard.

Mary decided not to run for reelection in 2006, but is seeking the 5th Congressional District seat being vacated by Ernest Istook. She won the Republican nomination, defeating Oklahoma City Mayor Mick Cornett in a runoff primary, in which she received two out of every three votes.

In the general election, on November 7, she faced Oklahoma City physician Dr. David Hunter, the Democratic nominee, and independent Matthew Horton Woodson. Mary ran an aggressive campaign, walking door to door and appearing on television with her message of "Faith. Family and Freedom."

She was elected to the fifth district congressional seat by over 60 percent of the votes, becoming the second woman to be elected a United States Representative from Oklahoma. Alice Mary Robertson, only the second woman in the United States to hold this office, was elected in 1921. A note of irony is Alice Mary Robertson was born in 1854 and one hundred years later in 1954 Mary Copeland Fallin was born to follow (if elected) in her footsteps.

A slogan Mary used for her 2006 congressional campaign is similar to the one used by Alice Robertson when he ran for Congress 70 years ago. "I am a Christian. I am an American. I am a Republican."

Billie Letts

Award winning author and Oprah's Choice

Billie Letts was past 55 years old when her first novel, Where the Heart Is, was published in 1995. The book became a bestseller, was featured on Oprah's Book Club and subsequently made into a feature film starring Natalie Portman and Ashley Judd. Her second book, The Honk and Holler Opening Soon, became the first book chosen for the statewide reading program, Oklahoma Reads Oklahoma.

Billie Letts' first book, *Where the Heart Is* had an unusual plot. A woman lived in a Wal-Mart and birthed a baby in the store. What kind of an imagination must an author have to write such a story?

"A very strange one." responds author Billie Letts.

Billie Gipson grew up as an only child in Tulsa. Her parents, Bill and Virginia, were young, still trying to grow up themselves. Her mother was seventeen and her father just a little older when Billie was born in 1938. Both came from poor families. Neither finished high school. Both worked long hours, so for a few years Billie lived with her grandmother.

Friends of her grandparents became an extended family to this self-described ugly duckling with buckteeth and unmanageable pumpkin-red hair. An uncle once told her she was "the only girl in Oklahoma who had a dog prettier than she was."

At an early age, she discovered the joy of reading and storytelling. She credits her grandmother, neighbors and a librarian for pointing her in that direction.

She soon read all the children's books in the library and moved to more advanced novels. In the fourth grade, she wrote a book report on Erskine Caldwell's *God's Little Acre*, creating quite a stir.

Billie began to see the power of words. At age nine, she decided she wanted to be a writer. This talent was confirmed when at twelve, she won a writing contest sponsored by a local radio station.

By this time, Billie's father had started his own company, Arctic Air Conditioning. Both parents managed the business and taught Billie the importance of hard work. They were proud when she graduated from Union High School in 1956 and enrolled at Northeastern State College in Tahlequah. She was the first in her family to attend college.

Billie carhopped, washed windows, and taught dancing, among other jobs, to help pay tuition. She became good friends with Mary Munn and Mary Jane Craig, better known as Ugh, who lived across the hall in the dormitory. They all joined Sigma, Sigma, Sigma Sorority and are still good friends.

Mary Munn Battenfield said of Billie, "We were close in school, then we all married and were busy raising our children and lost touch. At a reunion in Tahlequah, we made the decision to get together more often. Now that our children are grown and we have more time, our friendship has grown. Especially since Billie and Dennis have moved back to Tulsa. Our husbands are also good friends."

Billie met Dennis Letts, a fellow student, at

Northeastern. He had spent four years in the service. "He was older, handsome, and exciting," Billie said. They were married in 1958. Dennis's brother, Ray Don, married Billie's friend Ugh. Ray Don and Mary live in North Carolina.

During the 1960s, Billie put her own education and desire to write on hold while raising her family. Dennis received his Ph.D in English, two sons were born and the family moved to Durant, in Southern Oklahoma, where Dennis joined the faculty at Southeastern State College. Billie worked part-time to supplement her husband's modest teaching salary.

Billie completed her undergraduate studies, in 1969, at Southeast Missouri State College and in 1974 earned a Masters from Southeastern. She taught in public schools and at Southeastern until her retirement in the late 90s.

Through the years, Billie continued to write short stories, occasionally sending them to publishers. She taught creative writing classes at the college and English as a Second Language to hundreds of foreign students, including Vietnamese refugees. She later used that experience in developing a character in *The Honk and Holler Opening Soon*.

After retiring from the classroom, Billie gathered up her short stories, screenplays and what she calls "terrible poetry" and decided she was going to become the writer she always wanted to be. She attended writer's conferences in Oklahoma City, Tulsa, and New Orleans, where she had an unforgettable meeting with a New York agent. She showed Elaine Markson one of her screenplays and told her about the short stories she had been writing. Her husband called them *Tales from Wal-Mart* Her favorite of the stories was about a young pregnant girl who was deserted by her boyfriend in a small Oklahoma town. Four days after the conference, Billie received a call from Markson asking to see the Wal-Mart stories, which included *Where the Heart Is*. The agent advised her to expand that story into a book. Two year later, Billie finished the novel. She sent it to Markson in May of 1994. Warner Books bought the novel in June. The very next month the film rights were purchased by 20th Century Fox. Then foreign sales started rolling in.

The book is about a young pregnant girl traveling to California, who was deserted by her boyfriend in Sequoyah, a small Oklahoma town. Hav-

Billie Letts, Oklahoma Reads Oklahoma author, 2004. Photo, Courtesy of the Oklahoma Department of Libraries.

ing no money, she lives in Wal-Mart and has her baby in the store. Billie said the story came to her one day, when she was in the discount store and thought, *someone could live here for a week, a month, maybe even a year and never have to go outside.* "Then I came up with the idea of a girl hiding out there because she had no place else to go."

The book was published in 1995. Billie then began an extensive tour around the country. The book sold more than three million copies.

Stores everywhere stocked *Where the Heart Is* except for one major chain –Wal-Mart. The mega-chain discount store refused to carry it, fearing it cast a bad light on Wal-Mart. However, the power of Oprah Winfrey, the New York Times Best Seller List, the Walker Percy Award, and a movie contract made them take a second look. Wal-Mart ultimately not only sold the book but cooperated in the filming of the movie.

Having *Where the Heart Is* chosen for the Oprah Book Club was a thrill. Billie had been in California working on the screenplay and had gone home for a few days to check on her dogs and the house. The phone rang, an office assistant asked her to hold the line, and that famous voice said, "Billie, this is Oprah Winfrey."

Billie, in shock, chattered, "Oh, you wouldn't have caught me if I hadn't come home from California to check on my dogs," And on and on. She caught herself and they all had a good laugh at her shocked response. The television host then told Billie, *Where the Heart Is* was chosen for Oprah's holiday book club.

Oprah flew Billie and Dennis first class to Chicago. At the airport, they were picked up in a limousine, taken to Harpo Studio and then to lunch at, of all places, a Wal-Mart snack bar. Usually the guest author and four members of the book club dine at a swank restaurant while discussing the book. Instead, they ate hot dogs at Wal-Mart.

On the segment of the show known as Oprah's Book Club, guest critics are flown in from across the country to meet with the author and discuss the featured book. Billie became friends with her discussion group and flew them all to Oklahoma to attend the premier of the movie, *Where the Heart Is*. At the showing, Lieutenant Governor Mary Fallin presented Billie with a plaque and named the day, "Billie Letts Day."

After appearing on *Oprah*, Billie says her life changed. People recognized her when she walked down the street. Most of all she was amazed at the mail she received from young mothers or pregnant girls who related to Novalee or from people living in similar circumstances. She received so much mail, that a book was written by her author friend, Mollie Griffis, entitled, *You've Got Mail, Billie Letts*.

Billie said people like to believe there is a town like the mythical Sequoyah, where people are caring and look out for one another.

Appearing on *Oprah* broadened her audience and her sales but Billie appreciates Oprah for influencing her public to read. Billie has received letters from people who reported that, because of Oprah, Billie's book is the first one they had ever read.

She was pleased with the movie starring Natalie Portman and Ashley Judd. The film writers and directors worked with Billie to keep the film true to the book. Billie's husband, Dennis, played a supporting role as the Sequoyah sheriff.

Her next book, *The Honk and Holler Opening Soon*, also took place in Sequoyah but at a time before Novalee arrives. It provided an interesting cast of characters, including the café owner, Caney, a paraplegic Vietnam veteran who has not been out-side the diner since it opened. A Vietnamese immi-grant Bui Khanh, a Native American wanderer Vena Takes Horse, an African-American church leader Galilee, and assorted characters frequent the diner. Bui Khann was a composite of the Vietnamese stu-dents Billie had taught. She studied Native Ameri-can culture and poetry before inventing Vena Take Horse. Even her secondary characters have unique personalities. Customers at the diner include Peg and Bilbo. Peg suffers from emphysema and carries oxygen while her husband, Bilbo constantly smokes and blows the smoke above her head.

Billie's most noted skill is her characteriza-tion. She has a way of making the people in her stories become the reader's friends. Ten years after her first book was published, people still ask her "What do you think ever happened to Novalee?"

She has always been a people watcher. As a child, her family went to a bakery, bought a loaf of bread, spread the slices with butter they had brought from home, sat on the curb, and watched the people go by. Billie constantly made up stories about the strangers.

The Honk and Holler Opening Soon became the first selection for "Oklahoma Reads Oklahoma" a statewide reading and discussion program to cel-ebrate Oklahoma' s Centennial.

Billie visited eighteen communities across the state, many in rural areas. More than 2500 people attended her programs. She also spoke at the World-wide ProLiterary Conference, which was held in Oklahoma City in 2004.

Elaborate and unusual ways were created to welcome the famous author. Many libraries were decorated as diners serving beans and cornbread, some had jukeboxes, others sponsored Main Street

Parades. Her most memorable visit was being flown in a four-passenger plane to Guymon, where her host picked her up in a limousine. As they passed down the street, other cars pulled off the road in respect. Billie said she felt like she was at her own funeral.

Large crowds of fans attended the tours making the first Oklahoma Reads Oklahoma a success. Audiences found Billie to be friendly and funny.

Humor is very important to Billie. She always puts funny episodes in her books. For instance Mollie O. in *The Honk and Holler Opening Soon* mistook a tube of Ben-Gay for her toothpaste. Billie said that had actually happened to her.

Billie's third book, *Shoot the Moon,* is different from the first two. Taking place in 1972 in DeClare, a small town in Oklahoma, it concerns a mystery that has surrounded the town for years.

Billie does not usually plot her novels. She knows where she wants to begin and how the story will end, but the rest develops while she is writing. Sometimes, she's as surprised as the reader when her plot takes a twist.

Her fourth book, as yet unnamed is now being written. Billie has just emerged from a hotel where she has closeted herself for six weeks of dedicated writing. She has difficulty writing at home with all the distractions of telephones, repairmen, and household duties.

Billie and Dennis are proud of their sons, who are also creative. Tracy is an actor and playwright who lives in Chicago. Billie and Tracy have together written a screenplay for *The Honk and Holler Opening Soon*. He was one of three finalists for the Pulitzer Prize. He wrote the play "Bug" which ran in New York. The play was optioned for a movie and he was asked to write the screenplay. The movie, "Bug" will

open in December 2006. Dennis and Billie are looking forward to attending the premier.

Shawn is a musician/composer living in
Singapore. His four CD's have not yet been distributed in the United States.

Billie's stepson Dana is a librarian at Northeastern, and Billie says is a "computer whiz."

Fans continually ask Billie how to write a
book. She says she doesn't know. She simply has
stories to tell and begins typing.

Billie said, "The first time I walked into a
bookstore and saw, *my book* with *my name* on the
cover, I was ready to deliver the line I'd been saying
in my head since I was a kid: 'Now, at last, I'm a *real*
writer.' But I didn't say it because I suddenly knew
I'd been a real writer for almost fifty years."

Shannon Lucid, Astronaut. Photo, Courtesy of National Aeronautics and Space Administration.

Shannon Lucid

Space Pioneer

Shannon Lucid has logged more continuous hours in space than any other American astronaut, male or female. She spent seven months on the Mir space station in 1996 and was the first American woman to go into space five times. She was the first and only woman to receive the Congressional Space Medal of Honor awarded by the President of the United States.

The first year of Shannon Lucid's life was spent in a concentration camp in China. Fifty-three years later she spent seven months in outer space on the Mir space station.

She was born Shannon M. Wells on January 14, 1943 in Shanghai, China to missionaries Joseph Oscar and Myrtle Wells. Her parents had met and married while living there. Shannon's mother, Myrtle, had come to China as a girl, with her father. In 1940, Shannon's dad had fulfilled his mother's dream that her son would be a missionary to China.

When Shannon was only six weeks old, Japanese troops occupied Shanghai and took the family prisoners in retaliation for Roosevelt imprisoning the Japanese in America. Shannon's family, along with forty-seven other British and American prisoners, was incarcerated in two bedrooms at an old university. Reverend Wells was the cook for the concentration camp.

In a 1996 interview with *Oklahoma Today*, her father reported that Shannon grew up on rice, Cream of Wheat, and powdered milk that he obtained however possible. "My wife would take her portion of rice and mine, skim the worms off the top and mix the powdered milk with it to keep the baby alive. I weighed one hundred and eighty-seven pounds when we went in, and seventy-eight when we came out."

Shannon's mother told a reporter for the *Tulsa World* in 1980, it was their faith in God that kept them going. When they were released, a year later, all the prisoners were emaciated except Shannon. A doctor examined her and said "she looked healthier than children he saw in his office every day in New York."

When the family was finally released, they traveled on a ship built for 500, but which now carried 1,550 people to east India to be exchanged for Japanese prisoners. They were on the water for seventy-six days, avoiding mines.

The family ended up in New York, then lived in Michigan and Fort Worth, Texas. When World War II ended, they returned to China as missionaries under Chiang Kai-Shek's regime. By this time two more children had been added to the family.

When Shannon was five years old, she flew over China with her parents and younger brother and sister in an old Army transport plane. The plane was not pressurized and her siblings were sick, but Shannon was mesmerized. She later remembered thinking how remarkable it was that the pilot could fly the plane and land it on a small airstrip. She decided, right then she must learn to fly.

After the Communists took over China, Shannon's family was forced to flee, and settled in Bethany, Oklahoma. In junior high school she wanted to be a scientist when she grew up, which was unusual for a girl in the 1960s. The term astronaut didn't exist then but she wrote an eighth grade paper on becoming a rocket scientist. Her teacher told her to choose a more realistic goal.

In high school, she experimented with mice for a science project on cancer. She won local, regional, and national science fair awards for the project. She also received the Bausch & Lomb Science Award and the Oklahoma Junior Academy of Science published her paper on cancer. The National Science Foundation accepted Shannon to study at its summer and weekend institutes.

She graduated from Bethany High School with honors in 1960. Afterward, she saved up money from baby-sitting and house cleaning jobs to take flying lessons. She earned her pilot's license that summer.

She attended Wheaton College in Illinois before transferring to the University of Oklahoma. In 1963, Shannon received a bachelor of science degree in chemistry from OU. In most of her chemistry classes she was the only girl. She became a teaching assistant at OU's chemistry department in 1963 and 1964 and worked as a senior laboratory technician at the Oklahoma Medical Research Foundation from 1964 to 1966.

In 1966, she joined Kerr McGee in Oklahoma City as a chemist. It was there that she met another chemist Michael Lucid. They were married in 1967.

From the beginning, Shannon confided to Michael her dream of becoming an astronaut. He was supportive and agreed that if she was ever accepted into the program he would be willing to quit his job and move with her to NASA headquarters. However, Shannon didn't really expect that to happen as she had applied several times for jobs as a commercial pilot. Because of her gender she was always turned down.

In the meantime the aspiring astronaut became a mother to Kawai Dawn, in 1968, Shandara Michelle in 1970, and Michael Kermit in 1975.

Shannon served as a graduate assistant at the University of Oklahoma Health Science Center's Department of Biochemistry and Molecular Biology from 1969 to 1973 while earning a master of science degree and a Ph.D in biochemistry . She was working as a research associate with the Oklahoma Medical Research Foundation when she received the call saying she had been selected as a candidate for NASA's first group of women astronauts.

The new class of 35 astronaut trainees contained six women. Thirty-five years old, married and with three children, Shannon was not the typical class member. When asked by reporters how she felt about being one of the first women selected, she replied that she was not chosen because she was a woman but for her qualifications.

True to his word, Michael quit his job and the family moved to Houston close to the Johnson Space Center. He soon found a job as a chemist for a petroleum company in Houston. The children were exited, but disappointed when their parents told them they would not be able to go into space with their mother.

On June 17, 1985, mission specialists Shannon Lucid flew into space for the first time aboard the *Discovery* space shuttle. This eight day mission included satellite deployments for Mexico, the Arab League and the United States (AT&T Telstar). The Remote Manipulator System(RMS) was used to deploy and later retrieve the SPARTAN satellite which performed 17 hours of x-ray astronomy experiments while separated from the shuttle. The mission was accomplished in 112 orbits of the Earth, traveling 2,5 million miles in 169 hours and 39 minutes.

On her second flight, Shannon was a member of the crew of the Atlantis space shuttle from October 18, 1989 to October 23, 1989. As a mission specialist, she helped deploy the Galileo spacecraft on its journey to explore Jupiter, and performed numerous scientific experiments. The mission was accomplished in 79 orbits of the Earth; traveling 1.9 million miles in 119 hours and 41 minutes.

Once again, on August 20, 1999, she was on Atlantis for her third flight, a nine-day mission during which the crew conducted 32 physical, material, and life science experiments. The mission was accomplished in 142 orbits of the Earth, traveling 3.7 million miles in 213 hours, 21 minutes, 25 seconds.

In preparation for her future space endurance record, Shannon's fourth flight was a record 14-day mission on board the Columbia space shuttle, STSD-58, which was in orbit from October 18 to November 1, 1993. NASA management recognized this as the most successful and efficient Spacelab flight yet flown. Shannon and the crew performed cardiovascular, cardiopulmonary, metabolic, musculoskeletal medical experiments on themselves and 48 rats. This expanded our knowledge of human and animal physiology both on earth and in space flight. The mission was accomplished in 225 obits of the Earth, traveling 5.8 million miles in 336 hours, 13 minutes, 01 seconds. In completing this flight, Shannon logged 838 hours, 54 minutes in space making her America's female space traveler with the most hours in space.

She began training for the Mir rendezvous in February 1995, at Star City, Russia, learning Russian and going through several simulations to prepare her for the isolation of months in space with only two Russian cosmonauts to keep her company. Mir is the Russian word for "peace" or "world". The Mir space station was the world's first permanently manned space station.

Cosmonaut Elena Kondakova had spent six-months on Mir setting a new woman's space endurance record.

Shannon's record-breaking trip began with liftoff at Kennedy Space Center, Florida, on March 22, 1996 aboard STA-76 Atlantis. Following docking, she transferred to the Mir Space Station. Assigned as a Board Engineer 2, she performed numerous life science and physical science experiments during her stay on Mir. Her return journey was made aboard STS-79 Atlantis on September 26, 1996. In completing this mission, Shannon traveled 75.3 million miles in 188 days, 04 hours, 00 minutes, fourteen seconds.

She kept in contact with her family and events on earth through telephone conversations each week and a videoconference every other week. She also exchanged e-mail messages. Frequent media interviews were held by videoconference. She also carried a laptop computer loaded with training information, games such as chess, an extensive CD library, videotapes, music tapes, and a box of books, including a pocket Bible. Also aboard was a stationary bicycle and a treadmill to help her stay fit.

NASA only planned for Shannon to spend 140 days on Mir, but her return home was delayed twice, extending her stay by about six weeks. Her only complaint was the lack of books, candy and potato chips.

Shannon was the first and only woman to earn the Congressional Space Medal of Honor awarded by President Clinton. Russian President Boris Yeltsin awarded her the Order of Friendship

Medal, the highest award presented to a non-citizen. In 1989, she was inducted into the Oklahoma Aviation and Space Hall of Fame and in 1993 to the Oklahoma Women's Hall of Fame. In 1996, she was named "Oklahoman of the Year" by *Oklahoma Today* and is on the magazines list of "100 Notable Women of Style.

Before she left for Mir, the Oklahoma Senate adopted a resolution congratulating her for her role in the space program and wishing her well on her current space flight.

After her return, she was honored by the legislature and impressed them with stories of her six-months in space with Russians, America's former enemies. Later that day, she participated in a teleconference with several thousand children at the Omniplex in Oklahoma City, which was linked with 40 other Oklahoma sites. The event was also broadcast to schools nationwide by satellite. She lunched at the Governor's mansion with Governor Keating and visited Roosevelt Junior High School in Oklahoma City, where her brother John Wells, was a teacher.

She enjoys visiting with students and hopes her success will spark more interest in math and science among girls.

Between spaceflights Shannon's technical assignments have included the Shuttle Avionics Integration Laboratory and the Astronaut office at Kennedy Space Center. She has served as a spacecraft communicator in the Johnson Space Center Mission Control Center during numerous space shuttle missions and as chief of mission support and chief of astronaut appearances. She has traveled around the country speaking on her own experiences and the future of space travel.

Shannon has always been interested in stories of the pioneers of the American West. As a child, she wished she could have participated in those adventures. She never dreamed she would be a pioneer in space travel. She has said, "Space is perhaps the last frontier and I have been privileged to explore it."

Larita A. Aragon

Major General of the Air National Guard

Larita Aragon enlisted in the Air National Guard in 1979, to supplement her income as an Oklahoma City school teacher. She hadn't intended to break barriers or set records, but she ultimately became the first female general in Oklahoma history. As the nation's first woman commander of a state Air National Guard, she assumed command of the 137th Services Flight at Will Rogers Air National Guard Base, in 1989. This first woman to rise to the rank of general, in 2005, received her second star and was promoted to the rank of Major General.

Governor Brad Henry assisted General William Looney III as he pinned the two-star insignia on the epaulets of Rita's blue Air Force jacket.

"Once again, Oklahomans are setting the stage for the nation," the Governor said.

Rita is accustomed to being the first woman to achieve glory. However, it is a surprise that the petite green-eyed blond is recognized as the first female American Indian General in the military. While growing up, Larita Bly never considered her Native American heritage. In fact, it was a fact better hidden, and four generations of marriages with

Irish, Russian, German, and British made Rita's indianness inconspicuous. "I was taught respect for elders, leaders, and our land, but not for my Native American heritage."

When Rita entered the military, she made a conscious decision to declare that heritage. Her part-Choctaw father, Rhoper Bly, had been born in Colorado, and retired after 38 years as branch chief in the maintenance department at Tinker Air Force Base. Jimmie, Rita's part-Cherokee mother, was born in Alabama. She also retired from Tinker as an aircraft inspector. Rita's great-grandfather made the run into Oklahoma in 1889.

Rita was born in 1947 in Shawnee, Oklahoma, and grew up in the adjacent town of Dale, population 300. She had one sister, Connie. Although small in stature, Rita was an aggressive basketball player. After high school she attended Evangel College on a scholarship. In her sophomore year she transferred to and received her bachelor of science degree in education from Central State College in Edmond, Oklahoma.

Her first teaching experience was at Culbertson Elementary, an all black school in Oklahoma City. She said, "I'd never been exposed to children of color, and they taught me as much about their culture as I could have taught them about reading or math."

For ten years, she taught kindergarten through seventh grade at various schools in Oklahoma City before becoming a principal in 1984. She was named "Principal of the Year" in 1988 and 1992 and was selected as the Oklahoma City Chamber of Commerce Excellent Educator of the Year in 1990.

Her first husband, and the father of her two children was a church youth minister. They divorced, and she became the family's sole support.

Single for five years, Rita added to her teaching income by working at McDonalds and as a church secretary. A church elder, who served as a guardsman, suggested Rita sign up with the Air National Guard. He assured her they would schedule her to work when she was not teaching, and in this way, she could build a second career. Rita enlisted as an Airman Basic in the 219th Engineering Installation Squadron as a draftsman apprentice.

She said, "I fell in love with the people and the mission and found a new way of life. I immediately gained 1,000 big brothers who looked after my children and my welfare."

Lackland Air Force Base in Texas provided basic training. For her specific training, she was fortunate that Tinker was considered the engineering Mecca. At the time of her enlistment Rita held a bachelor's degree in education and a master's in counseling and was eligible to apply for a commission. She didn't, however, believing that commissioned positions should be attained by first proving oneself in an enlisted position.

On her journey to success she accepted every mission offered and volunteered for jobs no one else wanted. She gained the reputation of getting the job done.

Two years later, Rita received her officer's commission from the Academy of Military Science in Knoxville. She returned to the 219th as an administrative officer.

In February 1989, General Aragon became the first female unit commander in the Oklahoma Air National Guard when she assumed command of the 137th Services Flight at Will Rogers Air National Guard Base.

Still an elementary school principal, her military experience proved helpful in dealing with students. Both the Guard and the school system were supportive of her dual careers.

At the base, Rita supervised a number of areas including range officer, fire arms training manager and food service. During the Gulf War in 1991, she was responsible for deploying troops for active duty. Her unit was sent to Dover Air Force Base for mortuary training.

This was the first time in history women had faced combat, and Rita spent a great deal of time being interviewed. She was often asked, "What would you think if it was your daughter being sent to fight?"

Her answer: "The same thing I would think if it was my son."

Rita's worst nightmare came true with the bombing of the Oklahoma City Murrah Federal Building in 1995. Her assignment in the bombing recovery was that of Mortuary Officer. Her duties involved both body identification and family notification. The most difficult moments in her life were informing the parents of the children in the demolished day care center. Her counseling experience helped. During that time she worked 18-hour days between her school and duty station. The children at her school drew pictures that were later stitched into a quilt.

Recalling that fateful day, Rita said she was at a principal's meeting at the Oklahoma City Administration offices at 9th and Klein Street when she heard the bomb explode just a few blocks to the east. Her military training took over, as she told those around her to take cover. She ran out the south entrance to investigate, and was met by fire and the smell of smoke. News coverage had already begun by the time she ran back into the building. She immediately called her school, ordered them into lockdown mode and made her way across town.

Rita reported to her unit at Will Rogers Airport, where she was assigned to the morgue at the First Christian Church. She praised the professionalism of the notification team. She wore her uniform on family visits to provide an air of professionalism. What kept her going was performing a service that was desperately needed. She looked upon

Major General Rita Aragon. Photo, Courtesy of Rita Aragon.

it as a combat experience.

The Murrah building bombing was the defining moment in her career and in her life. Rita was relieved to get back to her children at home and at school. Opting to retire early from the school district in 1996, she went on full time active duty for the Guards.

On October 17, 1997, Rita organized 100 military women to attend the opening ceremonies of the Women in Military Service for America Memorial in Arlington, Virginia. Oklahoma was the only state to have a military group march in the opening ceremonies. The women were escorted in the grand opening ceremony by the adjutant general, the assistant adjutant general, and the chief of staff of the Oklahoma Air National Guard. State senators Enoch Kelly Haney and Kathleen Wilcoxson also participated in the dedication. Rita was instrumental in raising more than $18,000 for the memorial in the name of the women who had served in the armed forces from Oklahoma. For these efforts, in 1998, The War Veterans Commission of Oklahoma recognized Rita as the Oklahoma Woman Veteran of the Year.

In March of 2003, Rita was promoted to Brigadier General and named Assistant Adjutant General, directly responsible to the Adjutant General of Oklahoma for the supervision and continuity of all units of the Oklahoma Air National Guard.

From September 2003 to September 2005, Rita served a dual-hat assignment. She also was Air National Guard Assistant to the Assistant Secretary of the Air Force for Financial Management and Comptroller, based at the Pentagon, Washington, D.C.

She next served as the Air National Guard Assistant to the Commander, Air Education and

---

Training Command, the Air Force's second largest command, based at Randolph Air Force Base, Texas. She worked as assistant to Air Force General William R. Looney III, a former Oklahoma resident.

General Looney is responsible for recruiting, training and educating all Air Force personnel. His command consists of 13 bases, including Altus Air Force Base and Vance Air Force base in Enid.

The first woman to rise to the rank of general received her second star on December 22, 2005, at the state Capitol's blue room.

"I love wearing this uniform. I'm extremely proud to be a member of the United States Air Force and the Oklahoma National Guard. I am proud to be an Oklahoman, and I am proud to have all of you as my friends," the Major General said.

Brigadier General Harry M. Wyatt, the state adjutant general said "While we're extremely proud that she is the first female general in Oklahoma and the first that I'm aware of to command an Air National Guard in any state, she is being promoted not because she is a woman, but because of what she has done. She obviously is a very bright and talented person. It speaks to the opportunities available in the National Guard. It also speaks volumes about Rita Aragon as an individual that she took these opportunities and did something with them."

Rita credits fellow soldiers and others who have encouraged her. The best part of her job has been working with fellow airmen. She has never had a problem with being a woman who supervised men. "If so, not to my face," she laughs. " I have always worked hard and been fair, and was treated with respect."

Rita appreciates her husband, J. Greg Aragon, Jr. Her best friend, closest confidant, and strongest supporter, he keeps their home intact while she is away. "He allows me the flexibility to follow my dreams and goals."

The couple was married on April 11. 1982. He brought four children to the marriage and became an immediate father to her two.

Two of the six children also joined the National Guard. Her son, Greg Aragon III became Sergeant Major (E9) in the Nevada National Guard, and Rita's daughter, Dana Cortez and son-in-law, Jimmy Cortez, both serve under her in the Oklahoma National Guard.

Dana is a member of the 138th Medical Squadron stationed in Tulsa, and Jimmy, also an Oklahoma City Police officer, is a member of the 137th Medical Squadron.

Rita's job puts her in the position of sending soldiers, perhaps even her own daughter, to hostile areas. She addresses parents who send their children to war: "I have the same types of fears and apprehensions."

Even after twenty years of military service it is still painful for Rita to watch fellow guardsmen leave for combat. The separation is often harder on family members than on the soldier. "Guardsman are trained and ready to fight, but they still have spouses, children, or other family members left at home. As a member of the National Guard, you know what the reality is and accept the risk to step into harm's way to protect other people," she said.

Major General Rita Aragon believes she is the "poster child" for all women in the military. As guest speaker at the 2006 Women's History Memorial Service she spoke about the role women have played there. Women have served in the armed forces since the American Revolution when they were hired as cooks, seamstresses, scouts, couriers, medial specialists and even saboteurs. Their roles have continued to expand throughout the latter half of the 20th century, until currently women make up 15 percent of the active duty force and approximately 23 percent of America's reserve force.

Among the many awards Rita has received are: The Legion of Merit; Meritorious Service Medal with two device's; Air Force Commendation Medal; Army Commendation Medal; Air Force Achievement Medal; Air Force Outstanding Unit Award; National Defense Service Medal; Global War on Terrorism medal; and the Small Arms Expert Marksmanship ribbon.

She has been named the Woman of the Year for Government in Edmond; Oklahoma's Women in the News by the Oklahoma Hospitality Club; Redlands Counsel of Girl Scout's Woman of the Year; and Oklahoma Woman Veteran of the Year. In 2003, she was listed as one of the "100 Notable Women of Style" by *Oklahoma Today* magazine, and in 2006, she was selected a notable woman by the Oklahoma Women's Almanac. In 2006, the Air Force selected her as their candidate for "Women to Watch", an annual event sponsored by *Diversity Magazine*.

In 2006, Rita began a new job. In September, she was assigned as Air National ard Assistant to Air Force staff A-1 at the Pentagon. Rita will move to Washington but will keep her home here and spend as much time in Oklahoma as possible.

She doesn't have much time for hobbies, but she likes to play golf. Her greatest passion is spending time with her nine grandchildren. Two live in Oklahoma, two reside in New Mexico, two in Nevada, and three in Hawaii.

Rita attributes her success to being in the right place at the right time, wonderful bosses, the opportunities afforded by the military and loving what she does.

Governor Brad Henry and Kim Henry present the highway sign designating Checotah, the home of Carrie Underwood, American Idol 2005 to Carrie. Photo courtesy of Travis Caperton, Legislative Service Bureau, State Capitol.

Carrie Underwood

American Idol – Oklahoma Idol

 Television's 2005 American Idol, Carrie Underwood, took the nation by storm. Called America's Sweetheart, Carrie's face adorns magazine covers across the country. Nowhere is she more idolized than in her hometown of Checotah. Just ask any resident.
 "Carrie, she's the sweetest thing ever!"
 "Fame hasn't changed her at all."

 In a town of 3,400 people, it is not surprising that everyone knows Carrie Underwood. "She is probably the number one conversation right now," said Lloyd Jernigan, director of the Chamber of Commerce.
 The local ranchers at Katy's Café interrupt their daily breakfast talk of cattle and gas prices to discuss the latest news about their hometown star.
 Residents have their own Carrie Underwood stories. Ora Ledbetter, sales clerk at Sharps Department Store said, "I went to school with Carrie's grandmother. The whole family's good people. I remember Carrie when she used to crawl under the dress racks. She would stand in front of the full-length mirror and jump up and down. She is still just as down to earth and full of life as she was then."
 The checker at Wal mart held up a magazine, "Her mother was in yesterday with new pictures. Did you see the new *Country Music Magazine* with

Carrie's picture on the cover? She's nominated for four country music awards, you know."

Most Checotah shops display posters. Jack Williams at Williams General Store at Onapa passes out pictures of Carrie. He said, "She grew up just down the road and was always a happy little girl. I knew she had talent, but this was a one- in- a- hun- dred- thousand chance, and she made good."

The twenty- three-year-old Carrie won the Fox television network's talent search on the vote of a half million people. Checotah residents were upset that they couldn't get through the telephone lines to cast their vote.

A news reporter asked Carrie, "Is Checotah famous for anything besides you?" She replied, "Steer wrestling."

But steer wrestling and even the annual Okra Festival never brought sightseers to town the way Carrie Underwood has.

Major roads entering town display signs "Checotah, Home of Carrie Underwood, *American Idol*, 2004."

Carrie doesn't get home much anymore. Since achieving stardom, her life has become a roller coaster ride. In her official bio, she wrote, "I never thought any of this would happen to me. These kinds of things only happen to imaginary characters on television or in the movies, not real people."

As in the song Merle Haggard made famous, she was born, "An Okie from Muskogee," on March 10, 1983, to Stephen and Carole Underwood. She was the last of three girls; Shanna was twelve and Stephanie, nine. Both sisters are now elementary school teachers.

The family lived on a farm near Checotah. Her father worked at a paper mill and her mother was an elementary school teacher. Living in the country, Carrie climbed trees, played on dirt roads and cuddled her animals. Most of all she enjoyed singing. She began singing in church when she was three. In a fourth grade production, she was cast as Mother Nature singing to the animals.

Her grandfather, Carl Shatswell, said, "I figured she'd make something of it. She sang all her life."

Carrie persuaded her mother to take her to local talent shows, where she usually placed in the finals. Her taste in music was varied, as her parents liked "oldies", her sisters liked pop, and she enjoyed listening to country on the radio.

In high school she sang at school and church events, county fairs, and car shows, but mostly focused on her studies. She graduated from Checotah High School, second in her class, in May, 2001.

After high school Carrie felt that she needed to "be practical and prepare for her future in the real world." She enrolled at nearby Northeastern State University in Tahlequah.

Shy, she joined Sigma, Sigma Sigma, and credits her sorority sisters for bringing her out of her shell. During the summers Carrie sang at NSU's Downtown Country Show. This Branson type revue included songs, dance and comedy. There she learned about country legends like Patsy Cline and the Carter Sisters. She competed in beauty pageants at the University and in 2004 was selected Miss NSU runner-up.

Majoring in journalism and mass communications, she hoped to someday work behind the scenes for a Tulsa television station. She produced a student-run newspaper and wrote for the school paper, *The Northeastern.*

Friends and classmates told her she should try out for the popular TV show, *American Idol.* In her senior year she discovered tryouts were being held in St. Louis, just hours from her home. Her mother tried to talk her into waiting a year. Carrie replied that in another year she would have to have a real job. So her mother offered to drive her to the auditions. The rest is history.

A friend and her mother joined Carrie and Carole on the all- night drive. The tired group arrived at 6:00 a.m. in St Louis and needed to be at the stadium by eight to receive wristbands to be eligible for the auditions. Then they waited eight hours before Carrie had the opportunity to sing for the producers. She was invited back to sing the next day and the next. The third day she sang for the judges who chose to fly her to Hollywood for the actual show. Carrie had never before been on an airplane.

Carrie possesses a strong sense of commitment. When she passed the second round of *American Idol* auditions, she was told she now belonged to the producers and could not perform anymore until the contest was over. She said the final show for Northeastern University's Downtown Country show was the next week and she couldn't let those folks down. After much persuasion on her part, the producers finally said, "what we don't know won't hurt us."

Northeastern President Larry Williams appreciates Carrie's dedication. While in college, she spent two hours a week caring for his mother-in- law as a hospice volunteer,

After arriving in Hollywood, for fourteen weeks Carrie competed against twenty- three talented vocalists on nation-wide television. Watch parties were held in Checotah homes and the dorms at Northeastern. Fans across the country phoned in their votes and each week other contestants dropped from the show, one by one.

Simon Cowell, usually the cynic, praised her, saying he could not believe no one had discovered her yet.

On the March 22 show, Cowell said, "Carrie, you're not just the girl to beat, you're the person to beat. I will make a prediction, not only will you win this competition, but you will sell more records than any previous *Idol* winner."

Back home, a billboard was erected featuring the native daughter's picture and the caption, "Checotah Says Reach for the Stars Like Our Own Carrie Underwood."

On May 13th when the competition was down to three contestants, a parade was held downtown to honor Carrie. Eight to ten thousand people lined the streets.

Checotah and Northeastern University were almost deserted the night of the final competition as crowds jammed the Muskogee Civic Center to watch the finale on two big screens. Oklahoma's first lady Kim Henry attended.

As Ryan Seacrist announced the winner, red, white and blue balloons dropped from the ceiling of the civic center onto the crowd. In front of 30.3 million television viewers, on May 25, 2005, Carrie beat the last man standing, Southern Rocker Bo Bice, to become the fourth *American Idol.*

The next day, United States Senator Tom Cole of Oklahoma presented a resolution congratulating Carrie Underwood for winning *American Idol.* The resolution thanked her for being a positive role model. It also thanked her for representing the state of Oklahoma as "an intelligent, kind, considerate young woman" to millions of television viewers around the world.

Governor Brad Henry declared May 18, 2005, Carrie Underwood Day across Oklahoma. In August, at the state capitol, Governor Henry presented Carrie with a replica of one of the Oklahoma Department of Highway signs declaring Checotah as the home of Carrie Underwood. He said, "Her parents and several fans were on hand for the event. It was a touching moment. Carrie's eyes filled with tears as she accepted the sign, and talked about how much she loved Oklahoma."

As part of her title, Carrie gained a recording contract with Arista Records. Her first single "Inside Your Heaven" was released June 14th. It debuted as the first country song to hit number one on the Billboard Hot 100, and sold 170,000 copies in the first week.

Carrie traveled the United States singing to hundreds of thousands of fans on the forty-four city tour of *American Idol's Live!* Small children, teenagers, and grandmothers stood outside the Lloyd Noble Center in Norman for hours waiting for her to make her Oklahoma appearance. She thrilled the fans by saying, "It's so good to be home."

Carrie appeared on the *Today Show, Good Morning America, The View, Dr. Phil* and even yodeled on the *Jay Leno Show*. She was featured in *People Magazine*. She starred in commercials for Hershey's Chocolate and was the latest spokesperson for Sketchers shoes.

Her second single "Jesus, Take the Wheel" was released October 18, 2005, and soon reached number one on the record charts, where it stayed for six weeks, setting a record on country charts.

In October Carrie attended the Oklahoma Music Hall of Fame awards in Muskogee to accept the Rising Star award.

She appeared on Macy's Thanksgiving Day Parade and performed "The Star Spangled Banner" before Game 4 of the 2005 NBA Finals. She sang and was a presenter at the Country Music Association Awards, and was the first artist with just one single to do both. She appeared in TNT's "Christmas at Rockefeller Center" and "Christmas in Washington," attended by the President and first lady.

In December, Carrie was named "Oklahoman of the Year" by *Oklahoma Today Magazine.*

As predicted by her hometown fans, in April 2006, she was the biggest winner of the CMT Music Awards in Nashville, receiving trophies for Breakthrough Video of the Year and Female Video of the Year for "Jesus Take the Wheel". The CMT's are country's only fan-voted awards show.

While traveling, Carrie worked with her professors to complete her degree and University requirements for graduation. She graduated in May, 2006, from Northeastern State University. President Larry Williams was quoted as saying he had some pressure by *American Idol* to just give Carrie a degree but neither, he or Carrie wanted that.

He said, "We are an academic institution, and we're going to protect our academic integrity. More importantly, Carrie would never let us do that. She wanted to fulfill the requirements for graduation in all respects."

Carrie said in an interview with *Oklahoma Today Magazine,* "graduation is very important. I worked for three-and-a-half years for that degree and you never know what could happen tomorrow. I could, for some reason, never be able to sing again. Besides, every parent wants to see their kid walk across the stage, especially when all their money has been going to put them through college."

June, 2006, Carrie turned over her title as *American Idol* to Taylor Hicks. But Carrie was far from Idle. In less than a year Carrie gained the reputation of the hottest young singer in Country music. In the spring of 2006,she traveled the country as the opening act for the Kenny Chesney tour. In the fall she joined Brad Paisley's tour. She won a Teen Choice Award in 2005.

Less than two years ago, she took her first flight. Recently, she flew three times in seven days executing a superstar itinerary to: Las Vegas for the academy of Country Music, where she sang and won two trophies, Los Angeles to sing on this years *American Idol* finale, and to Nashville to get ready for the Chesney tour.

Carrie recently bought a house in Franklin, Tennessee, a suburb of Nashville.

The first year she is eligible for the Country Music Awards, she is nominated in four categories; female vocalist, the Horizon Award, best single and video award for "Jesus Take the Wheel."

Carrie said on *Carrie Underwood On-line*, "This is my first time to be nominated for the CMA awards, so to be recognized for four is a big surprise and an amazing honor." The CMA Award Show was held in November 2006. Before the telecast, Carrie was asked by a news reporter which award she would most like to receive. She answered, "Probably the Horizon Award because it is for new comers, and you are only eligible for a short time. She easily won that award.

Carrie also won the female vocalist award. She was up against such veterans as Sarah Evans, Martina McBride, and Faith Hill. She was surprised and thrilled.

Visibly shaken, Carrie said, "oh my gosh, two years ago, I was sitting at home watching these very awards, watching all these other people win and have the best night of their lives. And this has been the best year of my life. Thank you, fans. Everybody that had anything to do with this past year, thank you so much."

Carrie is also the poster girl for the "Read Y'all literacy campaign for the Oklahoma Library Association to increase awareness of library programs.

Despite her success she is still known as the *American Idol.* When asked if that bothered her she replied, "If not for American Idol, I wouldn't be here. I will forever be grateful to that show."

Bibliography

Jerrie Cobb

Books

Cobb, Jerrie, *Solo Pilot; True Flying Adventures of One of the World's Top Pilots,* Jerrie Cobb Foundation; Inc. 1997

Cobb, Jerrie with Jane Rieker, *Woman Into Space: The Jerrie Cobb Story,* Prentice Hall, Inc, Englewood Cliffs, New Jersey, 1963.

Darcy, R. & Paustenbaugh, Jennifer, *Oklahoma Women's Almanac,* Oklahoma Commission on the Status of Women and the Women's Archives at Oklahoma State University.

Haynsworth, Leslie and Toomey, David, *Amelia Earhart's Daughters: The Wild and Glorious Story of American Women Aviators from World War II to the Dawn of the Space Age,* William Morrow and Company, Inc., 1998.

Lee, Victoria, *Distinguished Oklahoman's,* A Touch of Heart Publishing, Tulsa, OK. 2002.

Tolman, Keith, Jones, Kim, Gregory, Carl, and Moore, Bill, *The Oklahoma Aviation Story,* Oklahoma Heritage Association, Oklahoma City, OK, 2004.

Welch, Rosanne, *The Encyclopedia of Women in Aviation and Space,* ABC-CLIO, Santa Barbara, Ca.

Articles

Howell, Melissa, "Jerrie Cobb, Quest for Flight", *The Oklahoman,* September 11, 2005.

LeWand, Nicole, "Women Aviators Recall Testing", *The Oklahoman*, May 1, 1994.

The Vertical File, Oklahoma Collection, Oklahoma Department of Libraries

Internet Articles

Geraldyn M. Jerrie Cobb, Pioneer Aviatrix, http://www.ok_history.mus.ok.us

After More Than Three Decades, Cobb Deserves Ticket to Ride, Http:www.floridatoday.com

Bertha Teague

Books

Darcy, R. & Paustenbaugh, Jennifer, Oklahoma Women's Alma-
nac, *Oklahoma Commission on the Status of Women and the
Women's Archives at Oklahoma State University.*
Teague, Bertha Frank, Basketball for Girls.

Articles

*Stratton, W. K. "How Bertha Teague Changed the Face of Girls
Basketball (and dumped the Bloomers).* Oklahoma Today,
January-February 1990.
Thompson, Mickey," A Tribute to Bertha Frank Teague", Ada
Evening News, *December 26, 1990.*
Tramel, Barry, "Girls Hoops Evolve into Action-Packed Compe-
tition." *The Sunday Oklahoman*, April 27, 1997.
The Vertical File, Oklahoma Collection, Oklahoma Department
of Libraries

Interviews

Betty Estes-Rickner
Omega Landrith Johnson
Ray Soldan

Kay Starr

Books

Darcy, R. & Paustenbaugh, Jennifer, Oklahoma Women's Almanac, *Oklahoma Commission on the Status of Women and the
Women's Archives at Oklahoma State University.*

Articles

Bob Burke, "Little Dixie's Musical Heritage," *Oklahoma Magazine of the Oklahoma   Heritage Association,* Fall/winter,
2003-04 , Volume 8, number 2.
"Kay Starr to Receive State Honor" *Daily Oklahoman*, Oklahoma
City, Oklahoma, 1976
"Oklahoma Music Hall of Fame 2002 Inductee Kay Starr Biography, Resolution from the Oklahoma House of Representatives.

Internet

http//members.tripod.com/ Kay _Starr/biography.html
Starr,Oklahomamusichalloffame.com

Interviews

Kay Starr, June 2006
Geneva Sarratt, 2006

Jeane Kirkpatrick

Books

Kirkpatrick, Jeane, *The Withering Away of the Totalitarian State, and other Surprises*, 1992.

Articles

Kramer, Michael, "The Prime of Jeane Kirkpatrick", *New York*, May 6, 1985.
Whelean, James R.,"Jeane Kirkpatrick; Ideals Come First", *Saturday Evening Post*, December 1994.
Vertical Files, Oklahoma Collection, Oklahoma Department of Libraries
Vertical Files, Stephens County Historical Museum

Internet

Encylopedia Britannica Profiles; Women who made a Difference: Jeane Kirkpatrick, http://search.eb.com/;women/article Accessed 8/24/2006
Jeane Kirkpatrick, From Wikipedia, the free Encyclopedia http:// en.wikipedia org/wik: Jeane_Kirkpatrick (accessed 9/20/2006)
Jeane Kirkpatrick,NNDB Tracking the Free World, http://www.nndb.com. people (accessed 8/30/2006
Jeane J. Kirkpatrick, Senior Fellow, American Enterprise Institute, http:// www/aei.org/scholars/filter.all, scholars (accessed 8/24/2006)

Interviews

Jeane Kirkpatrick
Buddy Campbell
Pee Wee

Mazola McKerson

Books
Darcy, R.& Paustenbaugh, Jennifer, *Oklahoma Women's Alma-nac*, Oklahoma Commission on the Status of Women and the Women's Archives at Oklahoma State University.

Articles
Carlile, Glenda "Born to Serve", *Oklahoma , Magazine of the Oklahoma Heritage Association.* Oklahoma City, Spring and Summer 2006.

Vertical file Oklahoma History Center

Vertical file, Oklahoma Collection, Oklahoma Department of Libraries

Internet Articles
Mazola McKerson, Oklahoma Women in Politics, http//www.ou.edu/special/alberctr/NLO/index (accessed 10/9/2006)

Interviews
Mazola McKerson

Doris Travis

Books
Lee, Victoria, *Distinguished Oklahoman's*, A Touch of Heart Publishing, Tulsa, OK. 2002.

Travis, Doris, *The Days we Danced: The Story of My Theatrical Family from Florenz Ziegfeld to Arthur Murray and Beyond"*, The University of Oklahoma Press, Norman, OK, 1999.

Articles
Althoff, Tami, "Norman 101-year-old is Last Zigfeld Girl", The Oklahoman, *Oklahoma City, Ok., November 11, 2005.*

Collins, Reba Neighbors, "Memoir Dances Through Life", *Sunday Oklahoman*, Oklahoma City, OK, April, 18, 1999.

Jones, Chris, "May We Have This Dance", the Oklahoman, Oklahoma City, Ok., September 27, 2004.

Kinetz, Erika, A Ziegfeld Girl Who Can't Stop Dancing", The New York Times, February 8, 2004.

Vertical file, Oklahoma Collection, Oklahoma Department of Libraries

Internet
Doris Eaton Travis From Wikipedia, the free Encyclopedia http:/ / en.wikipedia org/wik: Doris Eaton Travis, htrpp// en.wik..or/ (accessed 9/20/2006)

Interviews
Doris Travis

Oklahoma's Miss Americas

Books
Bivans, Ann-Marie, *Miss America, In Pursuit of the Crown,* Master Media Limited, New York, NY, 1991.

Carlile, Glenda, "Norma Smallwood, Oklahoma's First Miss America", *Petticoats, Politics, and Pirouettes; Oklahoma Woman From 1900 to 1950,* Southern Hills Publishing Co., Oklahoma City, OK. 1996.

Darcy, R.& Paustenbaugh, Jennifer, *Oklahoma Women's Almanac,* Oklahoma Commission on the Status of Women and the Women's Archives at Oklahoma State University.

Jayroe, Jane and Burke, Bob, *More Grace than Glamour; My Life as Miss America and Beyond,* Oklahoma Heritage Association, Oklahoma City, OK, 2006.

Lee, Victoria, *Distinguished Oklahoman's,* A Touch of Heart Publishing, Tulsa, OK. 2002.

Articles
Carlile, Glenda, "Oklahoma's Miss America's," *Oklahoma Today,* Oklahoma City, Ok.

Drummond, Bob, "Elk City Whoops!" *The Daily Oklahoman,* Oklahoma City, Ok., Sept. 7, 1980.

"Elk City is Proud", *Daily News,* Elk City, Ok. September, 1980.

Jayroe, Jane, "Miss America Shapes Up", *McCalls,* March 1996

McDonnell, Brandy, "New Miss America Crowned", *Oklahoman,* Oklahoma City, OK. February 26, 2006.

McDonnell, Brandy, "Miss America Thanks Fans", *Oklahoman,* Oklahoma City, OK, February 25, 2006.

Owen, Penny, "Crown Iced Miss America's Birthday Cake", *The Daily Oklahoman, September 18, 1996.*

"Sooner Wins Crown", Sunday Oklahoman, *September 17, 1995*

Vertical files, Oklahoma Collection, Oklahoma Department of Libraries

Internet Articles

Home Matters: meet the Host, Miss Susan Powell, Discovery Home Channel, http://home.discovery,com/fantsites/homematters /bios;spowell . Accessed August 2006.

Miss America, the Official Site, www: Miss America Organization. http:missamerica.org Accessed August 2006.

"Oklahoma City University's Three Miss America Statues, Jane Jayroe, *Miss America Spring 2005 online magazine,* http:www.missamerica.org/newsletter, September 2006.

Interviews

Jane Jayroe 1995 & 2006
Helene Jayroe-1995
Susan Powell- 1996
Vinita Powell- 1995
Shawntel Smith- 1996
Karen Smith-1996

Clara Luper

Books

Calhoun, Sharon Cooper and English, Billie Joan, *Oklahoma Heritage,* Holt, Calhoun, & Clark Publishers, Inc., Maysville, OK, 1984.

Darcy, R.& Paustenbaugh, Jennifer, *Oklahoma Women's Almanac,* Oklahoma Commission on the Status of Women and the Women's Archives at Oklahoma State University.

Luper, Clara, *Behold the Walls,* published by Jim Wire, 1979.

Articles

Dean, Bryan, "Clara Luper Corridor Designated", *Sunday Oklahoman,* July 16, 2000.

Dryden, Dave, "Clara Joins Northeast", *Daily Oklahoman,* September 1994.

McNutt, K.S., "Clara Luper honored for Civil Rights Actions", *The Daily Oklahoman,* August 21, 2000.

Robinson, Judy Gibbs, "Civil Rights History Told", *Sunday Oklahoman,* February 13, 2005.

"Tearing Down the Walls", *Oklahoma Monthly,* April 1979.

Vertical File, Oklahoma Collection, Oklahoma Department of Libraries

Vertical File, Oklahoma History Center

Interview
Clara Luper, July, 2006

June Brooks

Carlile, Glenda, "Heroines of Oil", *Oklahoma Today,* Volume 47,
    Number 3, July/August1997.
Darcy & Jennifer Paustenbaugh, *Oklahoma Women's Almanac,*
    Oklahoma Commission on the Status of Women and the
    Women's Archives at Oklahoma State University.

Articles
Fritz, Mary, "The Mad Ma'am From Ardmore," *The Sunday Okla-
homan*, January 18, 1981.
Robinson, Sheila J. "Ardmore's 'Mad Mam' receives Lifetime
    Achievement Award," *Daily Ardmorite,* September 15, 2005.
Selected newspaper articles from scrapbook of June Brooks

Interview
June Brooks

Wanda Jackson

Books
Lee, Victoria, *Distinguished Oklahoman's,* A Touch of Heart Pub-
    lishing, Tulsa, OK. 2002.

Articles
McShane, Bernice, "Wanda Jackson Still Belting Out the Tunes",
    The Sunday Oklahoman, November 9, 1997.
Triplett, Gene, "Rockabilly Royalty", *The Daily Oklahoman*, Oc-
    tober 19, 2001.
"Capitol Hill's Wanda Jackson to Receive Nation's highest Honor
    in Folk/traditional Arts", *Capitol Hill Beacon,* June 23, 2005.

Interview
Wanda Jackson, August 2006.

Internet Articles
Oklahoma Music Hall of Fame Inductees, Wanda Jackson, http/
    /www.Oklahomamusicalhallof fme.com/wjackson.html,
    (accessed 9, 2006).

Shannon Miller

Books

Kleinbaum, Nancy H., *Magnificent Seven: The Authorized Story of American Gold*, 2002.

Miller, Claudia Ann, *Shannon Miller: My Child, My Hero*, University of Oklahoma Press, Norman, OK, 1999.

Miller, Shannon, *Winning Every Day: Gold Medal Advice for a Happy, Healthy Life*, Bantam Books, New York, 1998.

Lee, Victoria, *Distinguished Oklahoman's*, A Touch of Heart Publishing, Tulsa, OK. 2002.

Articles

Shannon Miller, USA Gymnastics statistics –11-8-96.

Benedict, Marcia, "Like Mother, Like Daughter, Miller Comparison", *The Sunday Oklahoman*, May 10, 1998.

Clay, Nolan, "Olympic Gymnast's 7-Year Marriage Ends in Divorce", *Daily Oklahoman*, July 9, 2006.

Parrott, Susan, "Shannon Miller Given Olympic Welcome", *the Daily Oklahoman*, August 7, 1996.

Shottenkirk, Marcia, "From a Gold Medal Performance to a Double Ring Ceremony", *The Sunday Oklahoman*, April 18, 1999.

Soldan, Penny, "Miller's Wedding Party Filled with Champions", *The Daily Oklahoman*, June 12, 1999.

Tramel, Berry, "Shannon's Beaming with Olympic Gold", *The Daily Oklahoman*, July 30, 1996.

Vertical File, Oklahoma Collections, Oklahoma Department of Libraries.

Internet Articles

Shannon Miller, Com.http.//www.Shannonmiller.com/author, athlete, speaker, accessed 9-2006.

Wilma Mankiller

Books

Darcy, R. & Paustenbaugh, Jennifer, *Oklahoma Women's Almanac*, Oklahoma Commission on the Status of Women and the Women's Archives at Oklahoma State University.

Mankiller, Wilma, Foreword by Vine Deloria Jr., Introduction by Gloria Steinem. *Every Day is a Good Day; Reflections by Con-*

temporary Indigenous Women, Fulcrum Publishing, Golden
Colorado, 2004.

Mankiller, Wilma and Wallis, Michael, *Mankiller: A Chief and
Her People; An Autobiography by the Principal Chief of the
Cherokee Nation;* St Martins Press, New York, NY, 1993.

Articles

Abbey, Susannah, "Community Hero: Chief Wilma Mankiller".
The My Hero Project

Devlin, Jeannie M., "Hail to the Chief", *Oklahoma Today*, January-February, 1990.

Featherstone, Marion, "The Transformation of Wilma Mankiller",
Oklahoma Gazette, February 6, 1992.

Howell, Melissa, "Wilma Mankiller, A Voice for the Cherokee
Nation", *The Oklahoman,* July 23, 2006.

Pagel, Jean, "Mankiller's Friends Hope 'Fighter Can Beat Cancer'", Associated Press, 3-1-96.

Simross, Lynn, "Cherokee Chief Pushes Self-Help for Development", *Los Angeles Times,* September 19, 1986.

Stephenson, Malvina, "Wilma Mankiller Always Thrived on
Challenge," *Tulsa World,* Sunday , April 13, 1986.

Whittemore, Hank, "She Leads a Nation", *Parade Magazine*,
August 18, 1991.

"A Warrier Fights Back, Newsweek, July 6, 1987.

"Mankiller, Wilma P." *Current Biography,* November 1988.

Verticle File, Oklahoma Collection, Oklahoma Department of
Libraries

Internet Articles

Wilma Mankiller – Women of the Hall – National Women's Hall
of Fame, http://great women.org/women.

Wilma Mankiller former Principal Chief of the Cherokee Nation, Native American Ancestry, http://.powersource.

Wilma Mankiller, Wikipedia, the free encyclopedia, http://
en.wikipedia.org/wiki/wilma

Leona Mitchell

Books

Darcy, R. & Paustenbaugh, Jennifer, *Oklahoma Women's Almanac*, Oklahoma Commission on the Status of Women and
the Women's Archives at Oklahoma State University.

Articles

Rogers, Rick, "Leona Mitchell to Inaugurate OCU Hall", *The Daily Oklahoman*, September 18, 1992

Walsh, Michael, "Destiny Rides Again, Leona Mitchell's Career Goes Boom at the Met", *Time,* October 11, 1982.

"Enid Native Performs in Guthrie", *The Daily Oklahoman*, January 18, 1985.

Vertical File, Oklahoma Collection, Oklahoma Department of Libraries.

Internet Articles

The Official Homepage of Leona Mitchell, http://leonamitchell.com//home.htm. Accessed August 2006.

Hall of Fame to Induct eight Oklahomans,

Interview

Barbara Mitchell

Merline Lovelace

Articles

Fresonke, Julia, "Literary Ladies", *Oklahoma Magazine*, May 2004

Internet Articles

Merline Lovelace, Bio, http:// web.mac.com/merline

The best reviews: http:// thebestreveviews.com/author

Vertical File, Oklahoma Collection, Oklahoma Department of Libraries

Interview

Merline Lovelace

Ida "B" Blackburn

Books

Darcy, R. & Paustenbaugh, Jennifer, *Oklahoma Women's Almanac*, Oklahoma Commission on the Status of Women and the Women's Archives at Oklahoma State University.

Video of interview with the OETA – 1999

Articles

The Winner: Oklahoma City's Ida "B", *TV and Movie Screen.*

"Television exhibit to Open in State Museum of History", *Chronicles of Oklahoma,* November 1991.
File on Ida B at the Oklahoma History Center

Interviews
Ida "B" Blackburn

Judge Alma Wilson

Books
Burke, Bob and Painter, Louise, *Justice Served: The Life of Alma Bell Wilson;* Oklahoma Trackmaker Series, Oklahoma Heritage Association, Oklahoma City, Oklahoma; 2001
Darcy, R. & Paustenbaugh, Jennifer, *Oklahoma Women's Almanac*, Oklahoma Commission on the Status of Women and the Women's Archives at Oklahoma State University.
Cynthia Fuchs Epstein, *Women in Law,* New York: Basic Books, Inc, 1981.

Articles
Mitchell, Cleta Deatherage , Losing Alma, *Daily Oklahoman,* August 4, 1999.
Daily Oklahoman, Oklahoma City, 5 Jan, 1995, 28 and 29 July 1999
Norman Transcript 17, February 1982
Pauls Valley Enterprise 31, May1917
"Alma Wilson" Vertical File, Archives and Manuscripts Division, Oklahoma Historical Society, Oklahoma City, Oklahoma
"Alma Wilson" Vertical File, Library Resources Division, Oklahoma Historical Society, Oklahoma City, Oklahoma
"Alma Wilson" Vertical File, Oklahoma Room, Oklahoma Department of Libraries, Oklahoma City, Oklahoma

Internet Articles
Linda *D*. Wilson, *Alma Wilson,* Microsoft Internet Explorer

Donna Nigh

Burke, Bob, *Good Guys Wear White Hats, The Life of George Nigh,* Oklahoma Trackmaker Series, Oklahoma Heritage Association, Oklahoma City, Oklahoma; 2000.
Darcy, R. & Paustenbaugh, Jennifer, *Oklahoma Women's Almanac*, Oklahoma Commission on the Status of Women and the Women's Archives at Oklahoma State University.

Wise, LuCelia, *Oklahoma's First Ladies*, Evans Productions, Perkins, Oklahoma, 1983.

Articles

Jim Killackey, "Foundation to honor 'Treasures'", *The Oklahoman*, March 19, 2006.

Dave Parker, "Donna Nigh, The First Lady of Charity", *Today's Family, The Daily Oklahoman*, May, 15, 2001.

"Former First Lady Still Helping Others", *The Donna Nigh Foundation Newsletter*, September 1999.

Donna Nigh, Vertical File, Library Resources Division, Oklahoma Historical Society, Oklahoma City, Oklahoma.

Vertical File, Oklahoma Room, Oklahoma Department of Libraries, Oklahoma City, Oklahoma

Interviews

Donna Nigh
Bob Burke

Reba McEntire

Books

Darcy, R. & Paustenbaugh, Jennifer, *Oklahoma Women's Almanac*, Oklahoma Commission on the Status of Women and the Women's Archives at Oklahoma State University.

Lee, Victoria, *Distinguished Oklahoman's,* A Touch of Heart Publishing, Tulsa, OK. 2002.

McEntire, Reba, *Reba; My Story*, Bantam Books, New York, 1994.

Wooley, John, *From the Blue Devils to Red Dirt;The Colors of Oklahoma Music*, Hawk Publishing Group, Tulsa, Oklahoma, 2006.

Articles

Bushnell, Candace, "What Reba Did For Love", *Good Housekeeping,* July 1995.

Carter, Tom, "Singing A Satisfied Song", *OK Magazine, Tulsa World,* May 1, 1983.

Jenson, Kathryn, "Reba McEntire" *Oklahoma Today,* May-June, 1984.

Miller, Linda, "Country Music Star Debuts Fashion Line". *The Oklahoman*, March 21, 2005.

Wooley, John, "Reba McEntire's Still Country, But She's Trying A Little Something New". *Tulsa World*, November 13, 1988.

"Reba, Is There Anything She Can't Do"? *Florida Coast, The Magazine for Distinctive Florida Lifestyles*, Summer 2005.

Verticle File, Oklahoma Collections, Oklahoma Department of Libraries

Internet Articles

Reba.Com. Http://www.reba.com/news/latest/Newsarticle.

Interviews

Reba McEntire, July 2006

Mary Fallin

Books

Darcy, R. & Paustenbaugh, Jennifer, *Oklahoma Women's Almanac*, Oklahoma Commission on the Status of Women and the Women's Archives at Oklahoma State University.

Articles

Casteel, Chris, "Fallin Easily Wins 5th District Runoff", *The Oklahoman*, August 23, 2006.

Davis, Phyllis, " Lt. Governor Mary Fallin Just A Regular Soccer Mom", *Oklahoma Woman,* August 2000.

Springer, Denise, "Lieutenant Governor Mary Fallin: A Mom to Watch", *Metro Family Magazine,* August 9, 2006.

"Fallin Wins GOP Nod for Congress, *The Oklahoman*, August 23, 2006.

"Oklahoma's Women of Influence, *Oklahoma Family*, May 2000.

Verticle File, Oklahoma Collections, Oklahoma Department of Libraries

Internet Articles

Mary Fallin From Wikipedia, the Free Encyclomedia, http://en.Wikipedia.org/wiki/Mary Fallin. Accessed September 2006.

Biography for Lieutenant Governor Mary Fallin. http;/wwwok.gov/-ltgov/2003 releases/2003Bio.htm. Accessed September 2006.

Billie Letts

Books

Lee, Victoria, *Distinguished Oklahoman's,* A Touch of Heart Publishing, Tulsa, OK. 2002.

Articles

Collington, Jason, "Power Points, Oklahoma Novelist Billie Letts Has Found Where The Heart Is", *Tulsa World,* January 12, 2003.

Fresonke, Julia, "Literary Ladies", *Oklahoma Magazine*, May 2004.

Jones, Patricia Ann, "Mystery Rises Above the Moon", *Tulsa World*, July 4, 2004.

King, Dennis, "Hoot and Hoopla, Oklahoma Author Billie Letts brings the Pulse of Her State to Hollywood", *Tulsa World*, April 31, 2003.

Miller, Teresa, "An Interview with Billie Letts", *Humanities Interview*, Spring, 2004.

Verticle File, Oklahoma Collection, Oklahoma Department of Libraries.

Interviews

Billie Letts
Kitty Pittman
Molly Griffis
Bill Young

Shannon Lucid

Books

R. Darcy & Jennifer Paustenbaugh, *Oklahoma Women's Almanac*, Oklahoma Commission on the Status of Women and the Women's Archives at Oklahoma State University.

Haynsworth, Leslie and Toomey, David, *Amelia Earhart's Daughters: The Wild and Glorious Story of American Women Aviators from World War II to the Dawn of the Space Age;* William Morrow and Company, Inc., 1998.

Welch, Rosanne, *Encyclopedia of Women in Aviation and Space;* ABC-CLIO, Santa Barbara, CA, 1998.

Articles

Levy, Larry, "She's Come A Long Way", *Tulsa Tribune*, November 11, 2000.

Moore, Lonnie, "Shannon's Journey", *Oklahoma Woman*, November 2000.

Saucier, Heather, "Mission Accomplished: Shannon Lucid Fulfills Dream of Being Astronaut", *Tulsa World*, February 3, 1997.

"188 Days in Space, Down to Earth", Newsweek, October 7, 1956.

Woodward, Nancy and Devlin, Jeanne, "The Astronaut and the Olympian, 1996, Oklahoman of the Year", *Oklahoma Today*, December 1996.

Vertical File, Oklahoma Collections, Oklahoma Department of Libraries.

Shannon Lucid, vertical file, Library Resources Division, Oklahoma Historical Society, Oklahoma City, Oklahoma.

Internet Articles

Shannon Lucid: NASA Quest>Women of NASA, http:quest.arc.nasa.gov/people/bios/women/sl.html (accessed September 2006)

Astronaut bio: Shannon Lucid, http:www.jsc.nasa.gov/Bios/htmlbios/lucid.html

Larita Aragon

Darcy, R. & Paustenbaugh, Jennifer, *Oklahoma Women's Almanac*, Oklahoma Commission on the Status of Women and the Women's Archives at Oklahoma State University, "LaRita Aragon, Notable Women," p. 206.

Articles

Dean, Bryan, "Woman Makes History as Air Guard Commander", *The Oklahoman*; March 2, 2003

The Oklahoman, 27, March, 2003; 11 & 23, November 2003;

Whitaker, Lori, "Experience Can't Ease Pain of War," *The Oklahoman*, March 27, 2003

"Memorial Service honors Military, Civil Service Women," *The Sheppard Senator, An*
Authorized Publication of Sheppard AFB, Texas, March 22,

"Painting Honors Indian Women; 'Warrior' Model Serves in Guard," *United States Department of Defense*, Jun 30, 2006

Internet Articles

"Oklahoma Air Guard gets first woman General," *Army Times*, *www.armytimes.com*, 6/1/2006

"Oklahoma Air National Guard, Brig. Gen. LaRita Aragon, Proud of her Cherokee, Choctaw Heritage," *Army Times, www.armytimes.com,* 6/1/2006

"State's First female General Promoted," *Oklahoma's Military Stories,* www.newsok.com/military/ 1, June2006

"Brigadier General Larita A. Aragon," *Leadership.ucok.edu/ bio.files,* 11/14/2005

Oklahoma Air National Guard, Brig. Gen. LaRita Aragon, Proud of her Cherokee, Choctaw Heritage," *Army Times, www.armytimes.com,* 6/1/ 2006

Oklahoma Women's Veterans of the Year, *www.omd.state.ok.us/ OKWVO/recipients*

Vertical file, Oklahoma Collection, Oklahoma Department of Libraries

Interview
Larita Aragon, June,2006

Carrie Underwood

Articles

Davis, Sandi, "It's Good to be Home, American Idol: State Honors Checotah's Carrie Underwood", *the Oklahoman,* June8, 2006.

Davis, Sandi, "Surprise Visit Adds to Hall's Festivities", *The Oklahoman,* Friday, October 28, 2005.

Ibid, "Sweet Deal, 'American Idol' Carrie Underwood to Perform Jingles for Hershey Co." *The Oklahoman,* July 2006.

Ibid, "Oklahoma's It Girl'; Checotah's Carrie Underwood Dealing with Fame, *The Oklahoman,* August 5, 2005.

Painter, Bryan, "Pride Shows in Checotah," *the Oklahoman,* April 23, 2006.

White, Kathryn Jenson, "Carrie Me Home" – 2005 Oklahoman of the Year, *Oklahoma Today,* January, February 2006.

Wooley, John, 'Idol' Eyes A Show At Home", *Tulsa World,* June 4, 2006.

"Starring Carrie Underwood, Country Weekly, April 2006.

Carrie Underwood, American Idol, Oklahoma Magazine, May 2005

Internet Articles

Carrie Underwood on Line, http:www.carrieunderwoodonline. com/(accessed July 2006)

Carrie Underwood – Wikipedia, the Free Encyclopedia; http// en.wikipedia.org/wiki/Carrie_Underwood (accessed July 2006)

Carrie Underwood Official Site, http//www.carrieunderwood official.com/

Carrie Underwood, Great American Country, http// www.gactv.com